BEEN THERE, DONE THAT!

TRAVELS FROM YOUR ARMCHAIR

EWAN CARPENTER

INSIDERS' GUIDE®

GUILFORD, CONNECTICUT
AN IMPRINT OF THE GLOBE PEQUOT PRESS

Disclaimer:

Been There, Done That *is not a suitable source of information for you to feel in any way prepared to start any of the sports featured in this book, many of which can be very dangerous. If we've tempted you enough to get out and take part in these events, we recommend that you begin by seeking advice and instruction from qualified individuals—and, of course, get some comprehensive insurance.*

INSIDERS' GUIDE®

Copyright © 2005 by The Globe Pequot Press
(North American edition)

Copyright © Gusto Company AS www.gusto.tv
All Rights Reserved

Design and illustration: www.melkeveien.no

Library of Congress Cataloging-in-Publication Data is available.
ISBN 0-7627-3671-2

Manufactured in Florence, Italy
First Edition/First Printing

INTRODUCTION

Travel purges the soul, awakens the senses, and questions your very existence. But it's not for everyone. If you're agoraphobic or xenophobic, foreign travel might not be first on your list of pleasures. Some people don't have the money or inclination to travel and others can't bear the thought of leaving little Sparky the dog home alone.

This, however, is a book for those with cultural curiosity. It's for people who want to increase their own knowledge or impress others with facts and figures, local information, and global customs, perhaps without actually seeing them for themselves. For whatever reason—lack of monetary funds, a desire to convince others of your worldliness, or plain apathy—if you want world culture from your armchair, you're reading the right book.

We detail some of the greatest sporting events and festivals to take you to the places you haven't quite got around to visiting. We'll help you experience the passion, feel the adrenaline, and share the fascination of the players and the spectators of some of the world's finest sporting occasions. We'll even give you mementos to collect throughout the book and use in your own personal travel diary. OK, so you haven't really been there ... we won't tell anyone.

People are often pitched against adversity to provide others with entertainment. It's grace under pressure that arouses potent emotions. Within these pages we'll describe for you the greatest sporting events and festivals, often through the eyes of its most passionate fans and famous participants. We'll identify the heroes and explain the rules. And who knows, one day maybe you'll see it all with your own eyes.

So sit back in your armchair; the flight attendant will be along in a few minutes offering you drinks and checking your seat belt...

The tomato is a fine fruit. Most would agree it's a prerequisite for an authentic pizza, a core ingredient for a stupendous Bolognese sauce, the linchpin of a fresh salad, and it even has the courtesy to offer itself up for a good stuffing.

However, some people just aren't content with merely digesting this wonderful gift of nature. Their love of the tomato extends to wearing it, all over themselves, and making sure others get the same treatment.

If your passion for the tomato transcends mere sustenance, or if you just like being pelted with squashed fruit, then La Tomatina is the festival for you.

LA TOMATINA—THE BASIC FACTS

It's fiesta time in Spain. That means dancing in the streets, boozing, more dancing in the streets (with a lot less coordination), and eating truckloads of paella. But one festival is particularly messy, hosting the mightiest food fight of them all: La Tomatina. Here are the basic facts:

WHERE: The festival takes place in the Plaza del Pueblo in Buñol, Valencia, Spain. Buñol is only a short trip inland from the Spanish Mediterranean coast.

WHY: The fiesta is held in honor of the local patron saint, San Luis Betràn, and the Virgin Mary.

WHEN: La Tomatina takes place on the last Wednesday of every August, from 10:00 a.m. to 1:00 p.m. It is the pinnacle of the fiesta, which lasts throughout that entire week.

WHO: Some 20,000 people from all over the world descend on the small town of Buñol every year to drench fellow participants in tomato juice. The locals have had a bit of practice so if you're a wet-behind-the-ear foreigner, avoid the Spanish tomato throwers whose aim is as true as a laser-guided missile.

HOW: It's free and it's fun. Just show up to get a good soaking.

AMMUNITION: The variety of tomato is not the issue here. No one cares whether they're throwing beef, plum, or cherry. What matters is that 275,500 pounds of love apples are made available to the general public. Let the battle commence . . .

HOW TO GET THERE: Buñol is situated about 19 miles from Valencia, the nearest airport. Renting a car or taking a train from either Valencia or Madrid is straightforward. You may decide to go for a day trip as there's not much accommodation in Buñol, and don't forget to pack a change of clothes!

LA TOMATINA—IN MORE DETAIL

Fiestas are an integral part of Spanish existence. They're celebrations of life, religious beliefs, and traditions. Although it's something of a mystery just where the tradition of throwing tomatoes comes from, one event in 1945 could hold the answer.

THE BIRTH OF TOMATO THROWING

In the summer of 1945, as a carnival paraded through the Plaza del Pueblo in Buñol, some young bystanders decided to join in. But in their eagerness, they toppled one of the group of giant carnival figures. The giant rose from the ground, enraged and swiping at all those around him. In retaliation, the young ones grabbed vegetables and fruit from a stall and pelted the angered, stilted man. A food fight broke out, and La Tomatina was born.

In memory of the event, the following year, a crowd brought their own tomatoes. While at first the authorities were opposed to the juicy onslaught, they came to accept it as a new Buñol tradition. In 1959 it was officially recognized as a traditional Spanish festivity.

THE RULES

Preparations are completed and houses and shops wrapped in plastic sheeting by 11:00 a.m. when, in the Plaza del Pueblo, chants of "tomatoes, tomatoes, tomatoes" are answered by the sound of a rocket being fired into the air. The rocket contains the plumpest tomatoes, its contents splattering on the hoards below. It signals the start of the food flinging.

Of course, the temptation is to practice your pitching, combining accuracy and speed to hit where it hurts. But the organizers of La Tomatina try hard not to have their event turned into a violent brawl. The rules are as follows:

1. Remember what your teacher always told you at school: "You'll take someone's eye out with that." Always crush your tomato before throwing it.
2. La Tomatina is a noncontact fight. No shirt tearing or trouser pulling.
3. Only tomatoes in their natural form can be launched. Please leave glass ketchup bottles and cans of chopped tomatoes at home.
4. While ambushing the opponents from a high vantage point can be fun, don't climb atop the trucks carrying the tomatoes (ammunition).
5. When the second rocket is fired, you must put down your weapons.

PICTURE THE SCENE

Within minutes, locals turn from charming, honest citizens into marauding tomato grenadiers. The first shots are fired, usually at drunken foreigners, the town's inebriated invaders.

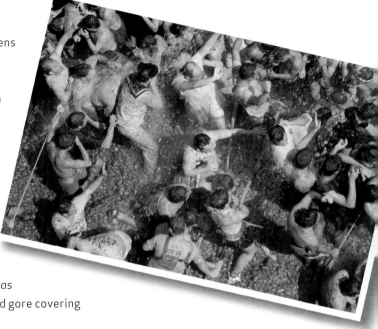

The trucks provide a continuous source of ammunition and soon the whole square is awash with tomato juice as Buñol rapidly resembles a scene from *Texas Chainsaw Massacre*, with red gore covering participants.

A flare at 1:00 p.m. signals the end of the fight and the cleanup begins, with streets and participants alike being hosed and showered down. The protective plastic is folded up, ready for the following year, and within a short space of time the town is restored to its pre-gunked state.

LEARN MORE
If you have an insatiable tomato fetish, contact Valencia tourist information. www.comunitatvalenciana. com (type tomatina in to Search).

5

FINNISH WIFE CARRYING

It's no secret that the Finns like a drink or two, so when there's an event where the winner's prize is his wife's weight in beer, you know it's going to pull in the crowds.

Finnish wife carrying has been celebrated every year since its revival in 1992 and in the past decade has drawn participants from all over the world. For most of us, wife carrying is performed either over the threshold and into the marital abode or on a wild Friday night after the bars have closed and the streets have emptied. The latter may be a good way to practice for the event, but here in Finland it's taken very seriously and training for the coveted prize starts early.

FINNISH WIFE CARRYING—THE BASIC FACTS

Most men spend their lives trying to get their women off their back rather than on it. Taking part in the Finnish Wife Carrying Championships requires you to carry your wife (or common-law wife) around an obstacle course. If you're really stuck for a female companion you can always borrow someone else's. You never know, at the wife carrying competition the woman of your dreams could be the one loaned to you, dangling off your back.

WHERE: The wife carrying event is held during the Sonkajärvi County Fair, starting in the Market Square. Sonkajärvi is a small town of around 6,000 inhabitants in the Lisalmi District in East Finland, a few hours drive from the Arctic Circle.

WHY: In the late nineteenth century, a thief named Rosvo-Ronkainen commanded a gang of thugs. He chose his men carefully after testing their strength and stamina in a contest. Like many of his countrymen at that time, not one for courting and wooing his ladies, Rosvo-Ronkainen liked his women plucked fresh from their beds in the dark of night. He and his men hoisted the women on their backs, transporting them from their villages to the thieves' hideouts. Modern wife-carrying participants have the good grace to return the women after the race.

WHEN: The event takes place each year during the first week of July.

WHO: Approximately 8,000 people attend the event, and it continues to win international attention. Qualifying sessions are now held in the USA, Britain, Ireland, Canada, Estonia, Russia, throughout Scandinavia, and even in South Korea.

HOW: Participants are charged about $60 per couple, although it's free for spectators. But if you're a red-blooded male you'll probably want to grab the nearest blond, swing her over your shoulders, and run like a wild man to claim your well-earned kegs of beer.

FINNISH WIFE CARRYING—IN MORE DETAIL

THE COMPETITION

If you take up the gauntlet and decide to carry, you'll have some stiff competition. In recent years, the Estonians, much to the chagrin of the Finns, have shown themselves to be true champions at this event. When they get a thirst on, they become inspired by the beer gods to thunder down the track, hair flowing and women clinging on for dear life.

With qualifying sessions now in place in numerous countries, you can expect the crème de la crème to be competing for Wife Carrier of the Year. For many carriers, their passengers are their secret weapons and will not be revealed until the start of the race. After all, it takes two to tango and technique is all important.

THE COURSE

The racetrack, located in the Sonkajärvi arena, was specially constructed for the event. It is 253.5 meters (832 feet) long and its surface is a composite of sand, grass, and asphalt. To make things a little less comfortable, there are a few obstacles to negotiate: 3-foot-deep water troughs, sand traps, and hurdles.

THE TECHNIQUE

In recent years the highly effective "Estonian Carry" technique has surpassed the more traditional fireman's lift. For the former, the woman squeezes her thighs around the man's face while hanging upside down on his back. Although to some this may sound like a pleasurable experience, maintaining this position for this distance requires strength and determination for both parties.

In addition, you must remember there is a 49 kilo (108 pounds) weight minimum. The weight is symbolic of the fine Finnish achievement by Armi Kuusela, the 49 kilo stunner who was crowned the first Miss Universe in 1952.

THE RULES

Choose your partner carefully. If you're a woman, you'll need the grip of a boa constrictor and a strong man to carry you. If you're a guy, a heavier woman requires more strength but equates to more beer should you win. Speed and technique are vitally important, but to avoid disqualification you'll need to adhere to the following rules:

1. The wife you carry can be your own, a neighbor's, or a complete stranger. Whoever you choose, make sure she's over 17 years of age.

2. Your wife's weight must be a minimum of 49 kilos (108 pounds). If she weighs less than that, don't expect to get off lightly. You'll be asked to carry a couple of sandbags to make up the weight.

3. The winner is the couple who completes the course in the shortest time.

4. If a contestant drops his wife, a 15-second penalty will be incurred, as well as a mouthful of abuse from his good lady.

5. Don't spend time building titanium, body-hugging wife scaffolding especially for the race. The only equipment permitted is a belt worn by the carrier.

6. The contestants run the race two at a time, so each heat brings you closer to the sweet beer.

7. The contestants are responsible for their own safety and security. So if you have a history of back pain, this may not be the event for you.

8. Contestants must adhere to the rules and instructions given by the organizers.

And the most important rule of all? Enjoy yourselves.

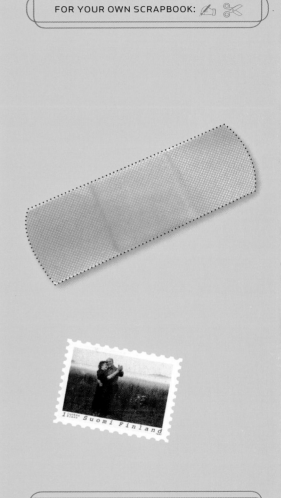

Suomi Finland

LEARN MORE
Contact the Finnish Tourist Board.
Tel.: +358 (0)9 4176 911
www.visitfinland.com

COOPERS HILL CHEESE ROLLING

Like something reminiscent of a sadistic television game show, the annual Cheese Rolling contest instills fear in its contestants. The morning of the race, in the aptly named Cheeseroller Pub in Gloucestershire, contestants are quaffing ale, their pre-race anesthetic, which they hope will mask some of the pain they're about to endure.

As the hour of the cheese beckons, they down their pints and troop to the top of a nearby hill, where they teeter, some already trying not to fall before the race even begins.

Spectators gather *en masse* to watch the event, as do ambulances and paramedics. Behold one of the world's strangest events. By virtue of its strangeness, it's also one of the most hilarious. Let the cheese rolling commence.

COOPERS HILL CHEESE ROLLING—THE BASIC FACTS

WHEN: The annual Coopers Hill Cheese Rolling race takes place on the last Monday in May, a public holiday. Races begin at noon.

WHERE: Coopers Hill is a small village near Brockworth, Gloucestershire, in the west of England.

WHAT: At 12:00 p.m., a circular Double Gloucester cheese weighing seven pounds is launched down a very steep hill and chased frantically down the slope.

HOW LONG: The cheese picks up speed as it rolls down the steep 600-foot slope making it impossible for anyone to catch it.

WHO: Anyone can take part. Not surprisingly it's the men who dominate this race, although there is a race for the ladies too.

HOW: To participate, simply show up. If you do decide to give chase, make sure someone is filming you. You'll look back on the action with great hilarity, provided there's no lasting damage from your tumble.

HOW TO GET THERE: The Cotswolds are approximately two-and-a-half hours from London and one hour from Bristol. Coopers Hill can be reached via the A46 road and is located between Gloucester, Cheltenham, and Stroud.

Chasing cheese down a hill is a strange enough concept. But with Coopers Hill's track record of injuries, it's frankly incredible that anyone would want to take up the challenge. In the past, authorities have tried to ban the event, particularly after 18 people were injured a few years ago, most with broken bones. However, a few years ago, in 2001 there was a record zero injuries—because the event was cancelled due to an outbreak of foot-and-mouth, a disease affecting cattle.

THE HISTORY

As is the case with many of the world's older and more unusual traditions, it's proven difficult to trace the origins of cheese rolling. Some talk of pagan rituals that involve sending burning wheels down steep hills to celebrate the coming of summer. Others believe that the practice dates back to early settlers, following the discovery of an Ancient

Briton fort at the top of the hill. The introduction of cheese to the tradition may have occurred more than 200 years ago.

THE RACE

It's 11:59 a.m. Like greyhounds with eyes fixed on the rabbit, competitors focus on the hulking cheese held back on a leash by a cheese controller. The huge Double Gloucester is goading them, it's flipping them the bird, whispering "I'm faster than

you, fat boys." The men are seething; they want to tear chunks out of that cheese. Win the race and they'll be able to do just that, as the cheese will be their prize. The master of ceremonies, wearing white overalls, a top hat, and a boutonniere, gains the attention of the competitors and spectators, shouting:

"One to be ready,
Two to be steady,
Three to prepare,
Four to be off."

And the race is under way, much to the delight of the crowd. The runners are off like a shot and some immediately lose their footing on the steep and uneven slope. Within the first five seconds, the majority of contestants are now rolling head over heels, like rag dolls being thrown down the stairs by a temperamental child.

Four thousand spectators gather to watch the races. Most hold digital and video cameras to capture the hilarity of grown men making idiots of themselves by chasing cheese hurtling through the greenery faster than a Roger Clemens fastball. This is a sight they'll want to show their grandchildren—"Look, that man there is your grandpa. He's cheese hunting deep in the English countryside."

THE AFTERMATH
Every year, medical teams stand by to tend to the wounded. One year alone saw 18 injuries—most suffered broken ankles and arms; some had more serious head injuries.

On rare occasions, the fun event has even ended in hospitalization for a spectator. Before the days of safety barriers, one watcher tried to dodge the cheese as it caught a divot in the ground and veered off in his direction. It hit him on the head, sending him flying down the hill and consequently into the back of an ambulance.

Upon regaining consciousness, he reportedly had a strange yearning to become a Green Bay Packer fan, but that cannot be confirmed.

If none of this sounds painful enough, why not stay around to try out some shin-kicking or wrestling the same afternoon? Once you've had a belly full of West Country ale, you'll be up for anything.

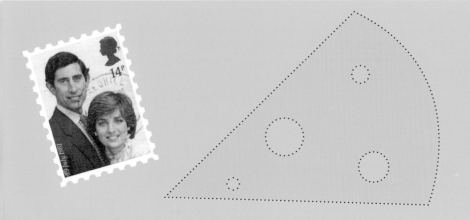

SONGKRAN FESTIVAL IN THAILAND

The New Year is celebrated three times in Thailand: Chinese New Year, western New Year, and Thai New Year. Each one is a good excuse for a party, but none more so than Songkran, the celebration of the Thai New Year.

This is a time of rituals and traditions and the ubiquitous sprinkling of water. However, walk through the streets of Chiang Mai during the festival and you'll see more than a dribbling of H_2O.

SONGKRAN—THE BASIC FACTS

Imagine yourself an unsuspecting visitor to Chang Mai in mid-April, excited by the imminent opportunity to sample a city full of Thai culture and traditions. You've heard the Thai people are wonderfully kind and gentle folk. It's been a long journey; you're starving and can't wait to dine on your first authentic *phad thai*.

You step off the air-conditioned bus into bright sunshine and a passing parade of the brightest colors. You delight in the fact that you've arrived at the height of the New Year celebrations. Digital camera at the ready, you take a shot of a beauty queen as she gracefully sweeps down the street, cheered by admirers.

Suddenly, a bucket-toting 20-year-old Thai man rubs talcum powder in your face and covers you from head to toe in ice-cold water.

It's time to get your revenge—at the world's largest water fight.

WHERE: Songkran is celebrated throughout Thailand, but Chiang Mai, a city of 160,000 people in northern Thailand, sees the most exciting activity over the four-day party.

WHEN: Songkran is celebrated for four days between April 10 and 18 each year. Each day has its own rituals.

WHAT: Songkran itself means "a move or change in the position of the sun." The Thai New Year marks the beginning of the new astrological year and is rich in symbolic gestures denoting a cleansing and a renewal of life.

WHO: Everyone celebrates Songkran, although it's the children and the young adults who get a more visceral kick out of soaking their friends, family, and, even better, complete strangers. More than 100,000 people are armed with water weaponry, so be prepared for liquid mayhem, which isn't such a bad thing when the average April temperature is 97°F.

HOW TO GET THERE: You can get to Chiang Mai from Bangkok by plane, train, or a 10-hour bus journey. It is linked to all main cities in Thailand.

SONGKRAN—IN MORE DETAIL

Many traditionalists would agree that the focus on the delicate sprinkling of water on religious icons has lost the popularity contest to the wholesale soaking of as many people as humanly possible. Some decide it's best to stay indoors during Songkran.

However, Songkran is supposed to be a fun festival for all ages, and Chiang Mai is a fantastic place to see exactly how the locals like to have a laugh.

DAY ONE

To cleanse and prepare for the New Year, the family splashes scented water on Buddha statues and images in their own home and in their temples. The younger family members sprinkle water on their elders as a gesture of respect and sometimes to ask forgiveness for the misdemeanors of the previous year (only a few hours away from committing fresh misdemeanors using their new pump-action water guns).

In Chiang Mai, the parades start with floats adorned with Buddhas and accompanied by musicians and beautiful local women wearing traditional dress. Needless to say, they all get drenched.

DAY TWO

Day two is dedicated to preparing the food for the traditional feasts the following day. This day, known as Wan Nao, is also traditionally the time to collect sand from the banks of the river, which is then taken by the bucketload to the temples. The sand is then molded and decorated with flowers to symbolize raising the level of the temple grounds.

DAY THREE

New Year's Day starts early as the prepared food is taken to the temples. The offering of food is done to "make merit," to ask for good luck for the coming year.

Officially, this is the first day of the mass water celebrations. And that involves you, as anyone can join in drenching everyone in sight.

DAY FOUR

This day is dedicated to the "pouring of the Songkran water," with respect given to ancestors and elders. This is the crescendo of the festival—within hours, the rituals are completed and the partying and water bombing are in full flow.

Between ceremonies there's always fun to be had, via food fairs, body building competitions, beauty pageants, and parades. Bars and clubs are open all hours.

THE HISTORY

The origin of the Songkran festival is ancient and has been widely researched. Those who have studied its history

X **Place your picture here**

X

believe that the Songkran started as a fertility ritual conducted each year by the pre-Buddhist Dtai people, some of whom still live in North Vietnam.

In Thai tradition, the phases of the moon and the lunar calendar play an important role in determining the Thai New Year. The word *Songkran* comes from the Pali language, describing a movement of the sun within the zodiac, from Aries to Taurus.

THE WATER THROWING — THE BASIC PRINCIPLES

You understand by now why water plays such an important part in the Songkran festival. But be forewarned: you'll get soaked, your friends will get soaked, and pretty much everyone in the city will get soaked. There's no way to avoid it, so leave your cameras and cell phones at your hotel. You'll be a prime target if you're on a motorbike or in a *tuk-tuk* (a motorized rickshaw). No matter how dangerous, a well-aimed water balloon in the face of an oncoming motorcyclist is the source of much mirth among the younger population who know no better.

You'll also notice the tendency to rub

white powder on the faces of others. This isn't some half-baked attempt at a Michael Jackson impersonation. It's to ward off evil and is usually smeared on by an elder. This simple scented powder will wash off easily—and fast—given the amount of water to which you'll be exposed.

THE RULES

If you can't beat 'em, join 'em. But there are a few customs to remember:
1. Don't ambush granny on her way to the temple. Respect your elders.
2. Don't water-bomb anyone in command of a vehicle unless you want to be mown down by a *tuk-tuk*.
3. Powder smearing should not be aggressive—always give the victim enough chance to decline your kind offer before plastering their face.
4. It's a noncontact sport and touching the body of a stranger, especially the opposite sex, is considered to be very discourteous—so avoid direct contact.

LEARN MORE
Visit the Thailand tourist board Web site at www.tourismthailand.org.

THE HIGHLAND GAMES

The global popularity of the Highland Games means that you don't need to go to Scotland to experience the traditions of the Celtic clans. Where there's a Scottish community, you'll be sure to find some form of summer games and the gathering of families. The games are particularly popular in the United States, where those of Scottish descent have kept the Celtic spirit alive by hosting their own Highland Games. From Alabama to Ohio, you'll find men savoring the smoky aromas of a fine Highland single malt, feasting on haggis, and tossing the caber, and in doing so, confusing the hell out of your average American.

THE HIGHLAND GAMES—THE BASIC FACTS

The Clanloddoch and Inverness Highland Games are two of the most renowned gatherings in Scotland. However, during the summer months, there'll be a whole host of games to attend in different locations throughout the country.

WHEN: From May to September, those residing in the Highlands of Scotland make the most of the fairest of months. The locals don their kilts and sporrans and, from the early hours of the morning until late at night, enjoy the competition provided by sports, dancing, piping, and, of course, drinking.

WHERE: The games are hosted throughout mainland Scotland and its many northern isles. The Clanloddoch Games and Gathering are held in Strathdon in the Grampians in August. The Inverness Games take place at Bught Park at the end of July.

WHO: This is an event for the whole family. It's a gathering of Scottish clans, and competition between clans is always very healthy. You may even be able to rub shoulders with the stars as the Clanloddoch Games and Gathering has been known to attract the odd celeb or two. Robin Williams, Steve Martin, and Ewan McGregor have all been spotted, although you're unlikely to see them tossing the caber.

HOW: To take part in the events, you'll need to register in advance. You can do this by submitting forms on some of the regional Highland Games organizer Web sites.

HOW MANY: The Inverness Games, one of the larger gatherings, has in recent years attracted crowds of up to 7,000 spectators.

HOW TO GET THERE: Fly to the Aberdeen or Inverness airport for best accessibility to the Highlands area of Scotland. The local tourist office will be able to point you in the direction of the nearest games.

Feats of strength and musical accomplishment are core ingredients of a successful Highland Games. Although the dancing and piping keep the crowds merry throughout the day, it's the Heavies who are greeted with the biggest cheers. These big lads take part in the "Heavy" events, launching missiles that an average man would have problems lifting. Rocks, axes, the lion's share of a tree—nothing seems too heavy for these boys to pick up and throw around the grounds.

THE HISTORY

The games are an age-old tradition of competition between Highland clans. It's been said by many that the feats of great strength and musical ability demonstrated in the modern games are reenactments of trials that a clan chieftain would ask his clansmen to perform in order to select his workforce. The strongest became warriors and defenders. The fastest became couriers, and the musicians helped pass the time, especially in the cold Scottish winter evenings.

The date of the first games is unknown. However, the games can be traced back to their revival in 1821 when organizers began to receive funding.

THE EVENTS

The Highland Dancing and Piping competitions are wonderful to experience and lend true authenticity to the games. Take part in the Strathspey and Half Tulloch or the Highland fling, both traditional Scottish dances that will put some color in your cheeks and a smile on your face as you're whirled around by your partner.

The crowd becomes rowdier as the Heavies step into the arena. Apart from the traditional track athletics, the field events are big crowd-pleasers as the strongmen test their mettle against objects of stone and wood. These traditional Celtic contests, sporting events that originated centuries ago and performed in Highland dress, still hold their appeal some 180 years after the revival of the games:

Tossing the Caber

The most prestigious event of any Highland Games. The caber is a tree trunk of up to 160 pounds in weight and is about 16 to 20 feet in length. Once balanced vertically in the arms of the carrier, it is heaved forward. It should spin in the air to land vertically, falling away from the thrower as it hits the ground. Guaranteed this is much harder than it sounds.

Weight Throws

It's distance that counts in this event. Swinging the 28- or 56-pound weight from side to side, the competitor builds momentum and releases the weight at the right moment to acquire distance.

Sheaf Toss

Hurling a bag of hay sounds like it could be a job for a farmer of the most diminutive stature. However, when the bag weighs 16 to 20 pounds and you need to toss it with a pitchfork over a crossbar, it becomes a slightly more arduous task.

Stone Throw

A *clachneart*, a stone weighing between 16 and 32 pounds, is thrown for distance. The stones vary in weight and are often an awkward shape, making it difficult to get any sort of grip. However, these men will have a go at anything.

Hammer Throw

A metal ball is attached to a wooden handle to create the hammer. It must not exceed one meter 30 centimeters (about 4.3 feet) in length and weighs up to 22 pounds. The contestant swings the hammer around his body in a circular motion to build momentum before he releases, desperately hoping it's going nowhere
near the crowd.

Battle Axe Throw

This event is about accuracy and distance. The axe is relatively light but must be thrown toward the center of a target.

FOR YOUR OWN SCRAPBOOK:

X **Place your picture here**

X

LEARN MORE

To take part in the Inverness Highland Games, you can register at www.invernesshighlandgames.com. For more on Scottish Highland events, head to www.visithighlands.com.

BOG SNORKELING WORLD CHAMPIONSHIPS
—GETTING DOWN AND DIRTY IN WALES

The British weather is unpredictable at the best of times. However, the summer of 2003 proved to be a great year for the esteemed British tradition of bog snorkeling. As temperatures reached record highs and millions of the great British public bathed in the blissfully cool coastal waters, a select group of "enthusiasts" were, of their own volition, wallowing excitedly in the filthy bog water of a small Welsh town.

BOG SNORKELING WORLD CHAMPIONSHIPS
—THE BASIC FACTS

WHERE: Waen Rhydd peat bog, south of the smallest town in Britain—Llanwrtyd Wells— in Powys, Mid Wales.

WHEN: The last Monday in August—a public holiday.

WHY: This is a charity event. However, there is, of course, the World Bog Snorkeling Champion title to compete for.

HOW: There is a participation fee of £10 (about $18). Spectators get to see it all for free.

WHO: Although one of the sporting calendar's filthiest events, it draws an international crowd. Previous years have seen competitors from the United States, United Kingdom, Australia, and Germany.

HOW MANY: Crowds of more than 1,000 can be expected to cheer on the smelliest of sporting competitors as they enjoy ice cream from Ben & Jerry's, one of the event's sponsors.

HOW TO GET THERE: Llanwrtyd Wells is in Central Wales and can be reached by train from Swansea or by car by traveling along the A483 to Llandovery.

BOG SNORKELING—IN MORE DETAIL

To participate in the Bog Snorkeling Championships, you'll need to make sure you bring your sense of humor as well as a gallon of liquid soap to kill the post-competition stench. It's guaranteed you'll have a laugh—and give the spectators a day to remember, too.

THE HISTORY

In 1986, a group of friends discussed how they could raise money for charity. Like many great British ideas, their concept of bog snorkeling was devised down at the local pub. No doubt the creative juices were flowing after a few pints of the local ale. Nearly two decades after its inception by organizer Gordon Green, bog snorkeling continues to be a great draw for locals, as well as national and inter-national visitors and the world's media.

THE COURSE

It's competition day and participants psych themselves up at the starting line. They focus intently on the muddy ditch that will be their home for the next couple of minutes. *Star Wars* fans often conjure up thoughts of Luke Skywalker training with Jedi Master Yoda in the stinking quagmires of Dagobah. Who knows what monsters lurk beneath the murky Welsh waters?

For the more grounded, the peaty bog and earthworms won't cause too much concern. They'll be intent on twice navigating the 55-meter-long (about 188 feet), one-meter-deep (3.28 feet) trench in record-breaking time. Tough new stand-ards have been introduced, resulting in a wave of the black flag and disqualification for anyone who doesn't make the first turn in 90 seconds. To achieve this means technique and strength are all important. No conventional swimming strokes are allowed, so whatever stroke is improvised will need to generate speed.

LEARN MORE
Llanwrtyd Wells Tourist Information
Centre Wales
0044 (0) 1591 610 666
Visit http://llanwrtyd-wells.powys.org.
uk/bog. html to download your entry
form.

For Philip John of Bridgend, Wales, a three-time champ having won in 2002, 2003 and 2004 (and knocking four seconds off the world record bog snorkeling time in the process), the prizes were a trophy and a year's supply of Ben & Jerry's ice cream.

WHAT TO WEAR

The beauty of bog snorkeling is that you can wear whatever you feel comfortable in. To most sane individuals, this would be a wet suit. However, as this is one of the least sane events you'll experience, anything goes. Some wear tutus, some their finest pinstripe cashmere suits. If you want to keep your job, just make sure you don't wear the same outfit to the office the following day.

UNORTHODOX BOG SNORKELING

Most would say bog snorkeling itself is fairly unorthodox. However, just to add a little more eccentricity, try the course on a mountain bike. Yes, there are specially developed bikes with their frames weighted down with lead. Riders also wear diving weights to keep them below the surface. Cycling down the ramp into the bog, their eyes settle just above the muddy water level. They must reach a pole at the other end of the trench, turn, and complete the second length.

Cycling is impeded as the tires slip on the muddy floor, but in a low gear and with enough strength, the bog can be mastered in just over a minute. Succeed and the coveted title of Mountain Bike Bog Snorkeling World Champion will be yours.

ANIMAL ATTRACTIONS

THE RUNNING OF THE BULLS
—BOOZE, BULLS AND BLOOD IN PAMPLONA

It may be part of your daily exercise regime, but if you live in the town of Pamplona, Spain, you've got to be seriously off your rocker to want to go for a run between July 7 and 14. If you do take to the streets, you'll be joined by a herd of bulls—and they're out for revenge.

However, if you're in Pamplona during that particular week, the chances are you will be tanked on red wine and afraid of nothing, let alone a bunch of wimpy bulls. And when you're in that frame of mind, anything can happen…

THE RUNNING OF THE BULLS—THE BASIC FACTS
The running of the bulls is possibly one of the world's most insanely dangerous sporting traditions. The spectacle is part of the festival of *Sanfermines*. Here are some basic facts:

WHERE: Pamplona, the capital of the Navarra region, in north central Spain.

WHEN: The bull runs take place at 8:00 a.m. daily from July 7 to 14, as part of the San Fermin festival in Pamplona.

HOW: Not surprisingly, those brave (or crazy) enough to run are mostly men. You must be over 18 to participate.

WHO: 700,000 revelers storm the city of Pamplona every year to experience one of the world's greatest parties.

COURSE LENGTH: 800 meters (0.5 mile).

DURATION OF RUN: A clean run will take approximately three minutes.

NUMBER OF BULLS DRIVEN THROUGH STREETS: six bulls and two steers, each day of the festival.

AVERAGE WEIGHT OF ONE BULL: 1,300 pounds.

FIRST BULL RUN: 1591, when locals joined in the moving of bulls from the corral to the town's bullring.

NUMBER OF DEATHS: 13 since 1924.

HOW TO GET THERE: The nearest major airport is Bilbao.

THE STAGE IS SET

The Fiesta de San Fermin starts at noon on July 6 each year. A flare launched from the town hall to signal the start of the festival is greeted by bugles, firecrackers, and screams from a delighted crowd. By 8:00 a.m. the next morning, you'll find the streets of Pamplona burgeoning with spectators and visitors. The running of the bulls, which occurs daily throughout the festival, is predominantly a test of male courage and seen by many as a "rite of passage"—those who take part as "boys" complete the run as "men." That is, however, if they complete the run.

The festival continues until July 14, giving you plenty of time to experience the joy, the tears, the exhaustion, and the celebration that nine days of boozing in the company of frenzied, party-loving Spaniards can induce.

RUNNING WITH THE BEST OF THEM

If you're a visitor, you don't need to sign up. Anyone, male or female, over the age of 18 can participate. But be warned, the only bull deterrent permitted is a rolled-

up newspaper—which will have little to no impact on a raging one-ton beast. Ernest Hemingway brought Pamplona to the attention of millions through his novel *Fiesta: The Sun Also Rises*. He loved the bravado and the sheer drunken mayhem that is the festival. Although women are allowed to run, they rarely do. Hemingway said once that "Pamplona is no place to bring your wife." If you're a woman or are considering taking a female companion, you might want to consider this quotation first:

"It's a man's fiesta and women at it make trouble, never intentionally of course, but they nearly always make or have trouble. I wrote a book on this once. Of course if she can talk Spanish so she knows she is being joked with and not insulted, if she can drink wine all day and all night and dance with any group of strangers who invite her, if she does not mind things being spilled on her, if she adores continual noise and music and loves fireworks, especially those that fall close to her or burn her clothes, if she thinks it is sound and logical to see how close you can come to being killed by bulls

for fun and for free, if she doesn't catch cold when she is rained on and appreciates dust, likes disorder and irregular meals and never needs to sleep and still keeps clean and neat without running water; then bring her. You'll probably lose her to a better man than you."

—Ernest Hemingway
FIESTA: THE SUN ALSO RISES, 1927

WHY ON EARTH?

The tradition of the running of the bulls began in 1591, when bulls needed to be moved from a corral to the town's bullring. The *encierro* (bull run) as we know it started in the 1600s, when locals got fed up with watching and decided to join in to help. It is one of the oldest and most exhilarating traditions in Europe, drawing huge crowds every year, ready to run for their lives or experience the intense carnival atmosphere. San Fermin is the patron saint of wine makers and merchants, which is why imbibing massive quantities of red wine has become such an important part of the festivities.

WHAT TO WEAR

It's customary to wear white on the big day. To really blend in with the locals, add a splash of red—as a neck scarf, bandana, or a sash around the waist. Along with the hundreds of locals and visitors who start the festival wearing white, by the end of the festival, soaked in Spanish red wine, your outfit will reflect the blood spilled by martyr San Fermin upon his death more than a thousand years ago.

NEGOTIATING THE COURSE

The course leads to the town's bullring, the scene of some of the festival's most exclusive bullfights and the very best *toreros*. Once the bulls have been driven here, it's likely they will die in ensuing bullfights.

If you think you can run like Ben Johnson and that stampeding bulls and steers chasing you down slippery, cobbled streets sounds like an exhilarating experience, this is the run for you. Bear in mind that while professionals run the 100 meters on a track, you're likely to be a novice and have 800 meters of twisty,

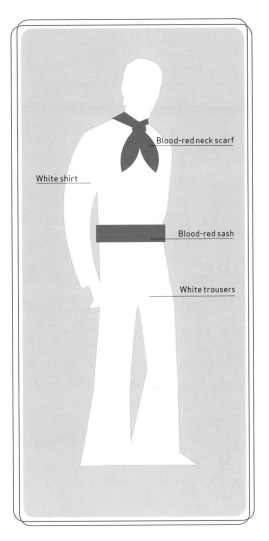

Blood-red neck scarf

White shirt

Blood-red sash

White trousers

look on in fascination and dread. First aid teams also stand by, and there's enough space between the lines of fencing for fence jumpers—those in trouble and in need of a quick exit.

A flare fired from the town hall signals the start of the run. Heavy wooden gates are thrown open and, in an explosion of immense energy, six angry fighting bulls burst onto the streets at incredible velocity.

The *Santa Domingo* is the first and most dangerous stretch of the course leading up to the town hall. Next, the *Mercaderes* requires braking into the corner and acceleration out of the bend. There's no protective fencing here, meaning a dire shortage of escape routes should you sense a bull's horn hurtling toward your posterior.

cobblestoned streets to negotiate. And remember, bulls can run twice as fast as men. Still care to go?

The *encierro* course allows you to join the madness at numerous stages over its three-minute duration. Think Formula One circuit: some corners are harder to deal with than others, while the straightaways offer you prime opportunity to put the pedal to the metal.

Double-fencing offers some security for both spectators and runners. Fencing lines the course behind which spectators

The final stages of *Telefonica* and *Callejon* focus the eyes on the finish line: the bullring. There's a narrow corridor before you get into the expanse of the ring, often causing human pileups and the most risk of injury and fatality on a larger scale. Once inside the bullring, the runners fan out to the sides as the bulls are driven behind gates to await their next outing and, more often than not, their demise. In this race there are no podium places awarded—your life is prize enough.

"There were so many people running ahead of the bulls that the mass thickened and slowed up going through the gate into the ring, and as the bulls passed galloping together, heavy, muddy-sided, horns swinging, one shot ahead, caught a man in the running crowd in the back and launched him in the air. Both the man's arms were by his sides, his head went back as the horn went in, and the bull lifted him and then dropped him. The bull picked another man running in front, but the man disappeared into the crowd, and the crowd was through the gate and into the ring with the bulls behind them … The man who had been gored lay face down in the mud."

—Ernest Hemingway
FIESTA: THE SUN ALSO RISES, 1927

If you're lucky (or unlucky) enough to get an invitation, there's a shorter bull run called the *encierrillo*, which takes place at 11:00 p.m. Unless you've packed your infrared goggles, your probability of survival has just taken a plunge the depth of the Marianas Trench.

THE TECHNIQUE

Experienced runners will tell you that in order to conserve energy, it's better to stay near the bulls at the start of the run, breaking away at the latter stages. This knowledge comes with age, and many of the men will run every year. Some of those who do return to run again believe their fear will have dissipated and that experience brings confidence. The locals of Pamplona will tell you that the more you have seen, the more you have to fear.

THE HORROR STORIES

With 13 deaths recorded since 1924, the most recent tragedy was in 1995 when a young American was gored to death. In 2002, at least six people were injured when bulls became separated from the

LEARN MORE
Contact the Navarra Tourist Office. Servicio de Turismo Gobierno de Navarra,
Edificio Fuerte del Principe 2,
4a Planta,
Plaza Tomás Caballero 1,
31005 Pamplona

herd. In 2003, three serious injuries to Americans and an Australian were recorded. In reality, the first aid teams will deal with more than 80 injuries in one day, although only the minority are serious. Anything fewer than 40 injuries is considered a "clean run."

And what is the major contributor to injuries and fatalities? Booze, of course. Many of those injured are inexperienced foreigners. They have never even walked the course, let alone run it, and hangover coordination isn't conducive to escaping a herd of furious beasts. Ever tried an early morning sprint with a hangover induced by a gallon and a half of Cava? No, I didn't think so.

ANIMAL RIGHTS

The Pamplona bull runs have always drawn the attention of the world's media and, as a result, groups campaigning for an end to what they consider to be the persecution of bulls. During the 2002 festival, animal rights protesters wanted to make a statement by running naked through the streets in protest. Local police, unperturbed, put it down to the party atmosphere—they'd seen worse sights in their combined festival years and didn't understand the protest slogans scribbled on signs in English.

VISITING THE FESTIVAL

If you're not a great runner, or have acute taurophobia, you can still enjoy the many thrills of the festival. It's largely lived by night. In fact, it's not unusual to hit the

streets at 3:00 or 4:00 p.m. having just risen to enjoy the evening's revelry. For many the 6:30 p.m. bullfight is the start of the day, with the subsequent hours offering ample opportunity to take in the street entertainment and music before dinner.

Following dinner, the town is yours to drink, sing, dance, and finally swagger home to steal as many hours of sleep as you need before the next day's drinking begins. Unless you're superhuman, you'll need to get some rest every now and again to make it through nine days of hard-core binge drinking. To help you hold your party head high, the bars rarely close, and when they do it's only for an hour or two to restock.

And for those of you who feel bullish enough to chant "you and who's army" at 8:00 each morning to the beasts with horns behind the heavy gates in Santo Domingo, we would suggest you replace this taunt with the following more appropriate prayer:

A San Fermín pedimos, por ser nuestro patrón, nos guíe en el encierro dándonos su bendición.

We ask San Fermín, as our Patron, to guide us through the bull run and give us his blessing.

THE SIENA PALIO

The Italians are known as a fiercely passionate nation. Visit Siena during the Palio and you'll see just how fiery their passion really is as the event stirs pent-up regional pride into frenzy. The Palio, one of the oldest horse races in the world, is a competition, a celebration, a grudge match, and a religious festival all rolled into one. These days there are few opportunities to experience a global event combining holy worship and financial skulduggery, all to see a team gain victory for its people.

THE SIENA PALIO—THE BASIC FACTS

WHEN: There are two races every year, one on July 2 and one on August 16. However, preparation for each Palio starts months in advance of the races.

WHAT: A race where horses and jockeys represent different Sienese districts, known as *contrade*. These *contrade* are in turn symbolized by objects and animals such as the Tortoise, Wave, She-wolf, Shell, Goose, Porcupine, Caterpillar, Dragon, Owl, Snail, Panther, Eagle, Unicorn, Ram, Giraffe, Forest, and Tower.

WHAT IT MEANS: The word *palio* itself comes from the Latin *pallium*, the name for the official banner that the winner receives on race day.

WHERE: Siena, a medieval city in Tuscany, in northwest Italy. It has 60,000 inhabitants and boasts incredible gothic art and architecture as well as one of the oldest universities in Europe, founded in 1240.

The Palio race takes place in the Piazza del Campo in the heart of the city, described by many as the world's most beautiful square.

HOW: You can try and squeeze into the Piazza del Campo for race day, but be prepared for a very sweaty and claustrophobic few hours. Many people are carried out of the square on stretchers, as the Palio is a law unto itself when it comes to the race start time. Chaos at the starting line has been known to result in postponement to the next day, if it becomes too dark to race.

WHO TO SUPPORT: Show an allegiance to one particular *contrada* and you could find yourself in a brawl. Things can get violent quickly between Palio rivals.

WHO: 50,000 Sienese will be cheering for their *contrada*.

HOW MANY: There are a total of 17 *contrade*. Ten horses race in each Palio, with the rear horse—known as the *rincorsa*—starting behind the other nine horses as the starting line is too narrow for all ten. The *rincorsa* gets a head start and is at a gallop before crossing the start with the other nine horses.

HOW LONG: Despite months of tortuous anticipation for the citizens of the rival *contrade*, the race only lasts 90 seconds.

HOW TO GET THERE: Fly to Pisa or Florence airport. Siena has good train links with all major Italian cities and is located off the A1 motorway.

To experience the tension of the Palio you need to understand the level of planning and preparation involved in the culmination of the July 2 and August 16 races. It starts as a well-coordinated event but the closer you get to race day, the more you realize the influence that money has on the winning of the Palio.

THE HISTORY

Siena fought long and hard to gain independence from Florence in the Middle Ages. Its *contrade* were designated to fund military companies to defend their city's independence. Each has its own church, patron saint, and museum. Today they defend and maintain their own identities with pride and often enmity. The Palio is hotly contested among the *contrade*, and ancient feuds continue to spur them on to beat their most bitter rivals.

The August race is an ancient tradition dating back to the twelfth century. Many believe that it descends from Roman military training. The July race, a more "recent" tradition, was first run in 1656. Of course, let us not forget that this is an event of religious significance. The races are held in honor of the Madonna of Provenzano (July 2 race) and the Madonna of the Assumption (August 16 race).

THE KEY PLAYERS

Months before the big day, a committee is selected to represent each *contrada*. The *captain* has financial responsibility in the days approaching the race, and his campaign budget is not inconsiderable. The wealthier *contrade* captains have up to $500,000 to play with. This is, after all, a serious game.

As the big cheese, the captain must also devise the race strategy. The *contrade* would do well to recruit some senior ex-Parmelat executives (think Italian equivalent of the Enron scandal and you'll get the picture), as corruption is the name of the game. Anything goes as they plot and conspire to defeat and humiliate their enemy.

The *barbaresco* is then chosen—he has the job of looking after his selected horse in the run up to the race and ensuring it is in prime condition for the jockeys (*fantini*) to ride to victory on the big day.

THE BUILDUP

The *tratta* contests prior to the big race allow the Sienese citizens to witness the drawing of lots to decide which horses will run. While each *contrada* may choose its own jockey, the horse is chosen for them. Ten *contrade* compete in each race, three of them in both July and August.

As the temperature gets hotter toward the summer months, so does the competition. Jockeys practice riding their new mounts and dress rehearsals get under way.

The night before the Palio, the Piazza del Campo becomes a racetrack coated with the golden earth, *la terra*, of nearby Tuscan fields.

THE RACE

"In the Palio, all the flames of Hell are transformed into the lights of paradise."
—Local priest Don Vittorio

At 8:00 a.m. on race morning, the jockeys can be found at Mass, praying for their protection and no doubt asking for forgiveness for the corruption they're likely to be guilty of before the race. The horses are also taken to the churches of the *contrade* they represent and are duly blessed by local priests.

So what happened to that $500,000? Scurrilous activity continues right up to the dying seconds before a race. Deals are forged as the horses assemble on the starting line. Race fixing at the Palio was grabbing headlines centuries ago. Horses have been drugged, jockeys paid off, captains bribed, steeds sabotaged ... this is Italian politics at its dirtiest.

As the horses approach the starting line, 50,000 nervous spectators in the Piazza del Campo scream for the horses bearing the colors of their *contrada*. It can take a long time for the horses to line up properly—some say a stalling tactic to steal more negotiation time for the jockeys.

Once they're lined up, the race begins. The jockeys ride bareback on their mounts, running three times around the plaza's 330-meter (1,083-foot) track. They're aggressive; they smell victory and whip anyone or anything that gets close to them. An incredibly tight turn, San Martino corner, has resulted in the death of jockeys and the broken legs of their mounts. The crowds whistle and jeer at their opponents and the cacophony swirls, along with the yellow dust from *la terra*, around the square.

Within 90 seconds the winner has crossed the line.

THE PRIZE

For the winner, adulation awaits. The first horse to cross the finish line, with or without a jockey, but most important with

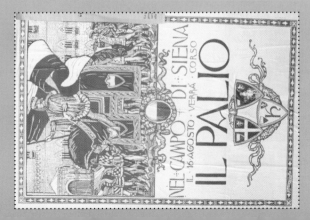

its face emblem still in position, is the victor and is swamped by the winning *contrada* inhabitants. This is one popular nag and will be the guest of honor at the evening's festivities.

Coming in second is deemed worse than coming in last—you're a real loser, having had the opportunity to win but not grasping it.

The winning *contrada* is given a hand-painted *palio*, a banner bearing the face of the Virgin Mary, and it's this *contrada* that gains the city's recognition of having earned the most importance. That is until its enemies plot its demise the following year.

LEARN MORE
Tourist Information
56 Piazza del Campo
Siena, Italy
Or visit, www.siena.turismo.toscana.it/
homeuk.htm

POLO—THE KING OF SPORTS

Picture yourself meandering past idyllic Gloucestershire villages among the richly verdant English countryside. It's a glorious day—the type of weather polo is meant to be played in. The sky is the deepest blue and, with the car's top down, you're blessed with the sun's cozy warmth and caressed by light winds. You cruise on, eagerly anticipating a glass of chilled bubbly.

Arriving at the polo club, you park next to Ferraris, Porsches, and Bentleys. (Forewarned that the glamour of polo starts in the car park, you've left the Ford Escort at home and rented a BMW for the day.)

In the cool shades of the marquee, celebrities glow as the champagne flows freely and, on the manicured field beyond them, a game of polo is commencing.

POLO—THE BASIC FACTS

There's undoubtedly something very special about polo. It's not just the handsome players; it's the excitement of the sport and the sheer elegance of the occasion. For polo's prestige extends to spectators and players alike. It's not called the King of Sports for nothing.

Polo is an exciting game and, beyond the very pleasant distractions of vintage champagne and exquisite food, it's a sport possessing a unique history—and highly skilled players to keep that history alive.

WHERE: Polo is played in more than 60 countries throughout the world, from America and India to Mongolia. However, the sport is best known for its bases in Britain and in South America, where it is most widely played.

UNITED KINGDOM

Polo's British headquarters is at the Hurlingham Club in Greater London, which hosts the Hurlingham Association International Polo Day, better known as the Cartier International, to contest the Coronation Cup.

Another famous British polo club is Beaufort in Gloucestershire, of which Prince Charles is a patron. Here, the Prince of Wales Cup is up for grabs.

Cowdray Park, situated in the beautiful South Downs countryside of West Sussex, hosts the Veuve Clicquot Gold Cup Final.

ARGENTINA

Most renowned among the many prestigious Argentinean clubs and polo training centers are the Argentine Polo Association and the Campo Argentino de Polo, in the Palermo district.

In addition, the town of Pilar, to the west of Buenos Aires, has a number of polo clubs and *estancias* (farms), where you can sample the less ostentatious side of the sport by attending a polo school.

WHEN: Polo is played mainly throughout the summer and autumn. It's from October to December, however, that three of the most prestigious events occur at Tortugas, Buenos Aires, and the Hurlingham Club. The Polo World Cup is also held every three years, in different locations around the globe.

WHAT IT COSTS: Attending a normal club game can cost around $50, affordable for the man on the street. However, access to many of the more prestigious tournaments comes at a far greater ticket price, through corporate invitation, or by having the right social connections.

To participate, a novice polo player will need to invest in a pony and pay for shoeing, stabling, vet bills, polo equipment, clothing, and club membership. All this could set you back a minimum of $10,000 in the first year.

HOW TO PARTICIPATE: Participating in a game of polo needn't be an unattainable opportunity. Many clubs arrange training days for members of the public, and at a reasonable cost you could find that you're a natural. It was Winston Churchill who said, "A polo handicap is a person's ticket to the world."

WHO TO MEET WHEN YOU'RE THERE: If you attend a major tournament, you're likely to mix with the rich and famous. Celebrities, supermodels, wealthy businessmen, and ambassadors from all corners of the globe rub shoulders, while bodyguards and undercover police diligently watch entrances and exits.

PLAYERS ON A TEAM: There are four players allowed on each team. These can be mixed, and there are many women now playing the sport worldwide.

DURATION OF THE MATCH: No more than eight *chukkers* (game periods) can be played in a match. Only six are played in a standard game. Each *chukker* lasts seven minutes with three minutes between them. A halftime interval of five minutes is also a requisite of every polo game. At appropriate moments in the game, spectators are invited to replace the divots flicked up by the horses.

FIELD SPECIFICATIONS: According to the Federation of International Polo, a full-sized field is 275 meters (about 900 feet) in length by 180 meters (about 585 feet) wide, if the field is fenced. Goals should be no less than 230 meters (about 755 feet) apart. Their width should be no more than 7.3 meters (about 24 feet), and their height should be at least 3 meters (about 10 feet).

POLO—IN MORE DETAIL

Polo is a fast-paced, majestic, and exhilarating game. Dexterity and skill are imperative as it is played at great speed. While polo is a dangerous game, those who do it regularly become addicted to the adrenaline rush of participating in an intense sport mounted on incredibly agile animals that can pirouette on the spot under command.

THE HISTORY

It is thought that polo may have been in existence as early as 600 B.C. The evidence comes from the writings of an early Persian poet; later the game's popularity spread through Asia. The ball, originally made from the root of the willow tree, was called *pulu*.

There are some who proclaim that polo originated with warriors on horseback knocking about a goat's head in their own backyard. But it wasn't until the 1850s that the British cavalry, with nothing better to do, compiled the first rules of polo. In 1869, the game was established in England, albeit played using walking sticks and a billiard ball. As its popularity increased, the Hurlingham Club was established in 1886, to govern the game and help standardize the rules.

Polo was taken to Argentina at the end of the nineteenth century by English and Irish engineers and ranchers, and the first official match there took place on September 3, 1875.

Since the 1930s, Argentina has become a force to be reckoned with, providing six of the world's 10 handicap players.

THE PLAYERS

There are currently more than 160 British-born professional polo players, accompanied by some 200 more international stars that also compete on British teams. Of course, polo's royal credentials come courtesy of three of its most celebrated players—the Prince of Wales and his two sons, Prince Harry and Prince William.

Polo players are ranked according to handicap, ranging from minus two goals to plus 10 goals for the best of the best. The highest ranking professional players will be paid big salaries often similar to those of other professional athletes.

THEIR PONIES

The polo pony is a horse of incredible agility and finesse. At first, the height of the pony was limited to 14 hands. However, now there is no such rule and an average polo pony measures 15 hands.

Since 1930, the best ponies have been bred in Argentina where thoroughbreds are crossed with the indigenous *Criollo* horses. Argentinean ponies have a reputation for the best conformation (the general shape of a horse, which dictates their strength and composure), as well as a superior temperament. The Aston Martin DB9 of the species, the Argentinean ponies' acceleration and supreme handling make them the envy of every polo player.

During a game, ponies wear bandages around each leg to

prevent injury from blows by the players' mallets.

EQUIPMENT

If you're a star of the polo world, you need to look the part. A pair of Ray Bans and leather driving gloves won't cut it. The following is the essential kit for a professional polo player:

- A helmet, complete with face guard and chin strap;
- Brown leather boots;
- Gloves to prevent friction burns using the mallet;
- Knee guards;
- A mallet 48 to 54 inches long, depending on the reach of rider and height of pony, and generally made of maple or bamboo;
- A thin whip; and
- Blunted spurs.

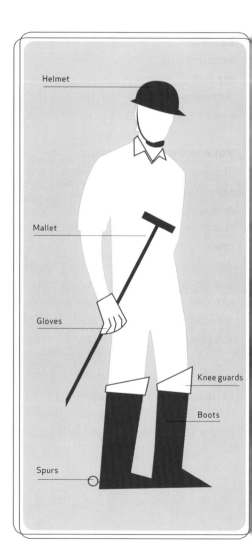

Helmet

Mallet

Gloves

Knee guards

Boots

Spurs

Each team wears polo shirts of distinguishing colors. At a charity event, the sweaty remnants are likely to be auctioned off—much to the delight of the female fans.

POLO WITH A DIFFERENCE

Thanks to new investment, Mongolia has seen a renaissance of the sport. In the land where polo arguably originated, players are using ancient methods to make their equipment. Mongolia's players who are skilled riders and hardy competitors (with even hardier ponies) are polo naturals, and many believe that, given time and training, they will be competing at a high international level.

In India and Nepal, elephant polo has become a natural extension of the game, and visitors to these countries can take part in a game with the well-versed locals.

LEARN MORE

For more on polo, visit the Hurlingham Polo Association Web site at www.hpa-polo.co.uk or the United States Polo Association at www.us-polo.org. Want to know more about the less conventional elephant polo? Then go to www.elephantpolo.com.

Las Vegas, Nevada, is a city where extravagance and hedonism are the rules of attraction. Some call it one of the wonders of the modern world. It's like an alien spaceship landed in the middle of the desert, its bright lights beckoning you to come aboard. Once inside, you're surrounded by a neon fantasy. And everyone's there to sample the fun. The grandparents are shoveling quarters into slot machines, and Dad and Mom are at the blackjack table.

In December, the cowboys come to town, riding into Vegas out of the desert, whooping and yee-ha-ing their way into the heart of the city lights as the sun dies behind them. It's a living enactment of the Shakespearean theme of the meeting of rural and urban. And if it's a simple tale of man against beast you're interested in, you've come to the right place.

NATIONAL FINALS RODEO—THE BASIC FACTS

WHAT: The Wrangler NFR, National Finals Rodeo—described as the Super Bowl of Rodeo.

WHEN: The competition runs for 10 days during the first two weeks of December. In 2004 Las Vegas marked its 20th anniversary as host of the event.

WHERE: The Thomas & Mack Center in Las Vegas, Nevada.

WHO: The greatest rodeo athletes representing their home states, and the toughest and hardiest livestock.

HOW: Tickets are in great demand for this sold-out event. Bear in mind that of the 1.5 million tickets demanded, only 40,000 are distributed to the public, with the majority of seats reserved for riders and their families and sponsors. You can seek tickets online or via the public lottery—but be prepared to be persistent.

HOW MUCH: Ticket prices vary. Expect to pay anywhere between $35 and $600, depending on which day you attend.

HOW MANY: More than 175,000 people come to the stadium over the two weeks to watch cowboys and cowgirls. In addition, more than 13 million viewers tune in, as all 10 events are televised.

HOW TO GET THERE: The Thomas & Mack Center is located on the campus of the University of Nevada, Las Vegas.

THE PRIZE PURSE: There's big money at stake— $5 million in prize money.

CAREER EARNING LEADERS: Joe Beaver won $2,362,361 through 2003. A rookie in the 1985 first Vegas Rodeo, Beaver was an unknown, but winning the championship that year and successive accolades has made him a big name on the circuit.

YOUNGEST RODEO CHAMPION: Jim Rodriguez Jr. won the championship in 1959 at age 18.

The NFR is the culmination of the rodeo season. It's the ultimate occasion for cowboys and cowgirls to demonstrate their skills in front of paying spectators and television viewers. The sport has matured greatly over the past decade, with serious money up for grabs and a new generation of fans. Animal breeding techniques have produced prime bucking stock, resulting in events that are more exciting for the fans and more challenging for the riders.

THE HISTORY

The first NFR was held at the Dallas State Fair Grounds in 1959 when Jim Shoulders, the hero of this era of the sport, won the initial prize purse of $50,000. While rodeo has always been a fast-paced, high-energy sport, it wasn't until later years that media interest developed and rodeo won more widespread appeal. Perhaps the leap in prize money following a move to showtown Las Vegas had something to do with it.

In 1985, Las Vegas staged the NFR for the first time, after 20 years in Oklahoma City. Herb McDonald and Benny Binion, the two masterminds behind its interstate transfer, continued to bring millions of dollars into Las Vegas through incredible ticket sales and sponsorship deals. Almost 20 years later, Las Vegas remains the natural host of the event and the two words "Vegas" and "rodeo" are inextricably tied.

THE EVENTS

Rodeo, the riding of wild horses and bulls, comprises several different, timed events. There are seven officially recognized throughout North America.

Bull Riding

This is the rodeo's most popular event. Mounting an angry bull is difficult enough, but once it lurches through the gates into the arena, staying on for eight seconds becomes a near impossibility. But staying on as long as possible is the goal, and many do last a matter of seconds before being slammed to the ground. If they are thrown, rodeo clowns will come to the cowboy's rescue. This dangerous event frequently results in broken ribs and limbs.

Steer Wrestling

This is one fast event, requiring accuracy and great physical strength. As the steer is loaded into a *roping chute,* the rider waits, mounted on a horse behind a barrier. As soon as the steer is released, the horse is spurred into action and the rider charges after the steer, leaping from his own horse to tackle the steer head-on. With the aggression of a football player, he downs his opponent and the clock is

stopped. The event is over within a matter of seconds.

Team Roping

This difficult and hazardous event can end in serious injury if not executed to perfection. It requires lots of practice to ensure the *header* and the *heeler,* both on horseback, work as a team. The *header* is in charge of roping the horns of the steer while the *heeler* waits for the appropriate moment to rope the rear legs.

The *header* makes his catch and winds the rope around the saddle horn. As he does so the steer is turned at an awkward angle, causing the back legs to rise in the air. This is when the *heeler* quickly loops the rope around the steer's heels. When both have completed their tasks, turning their horses to face the steer and pulling the ropes taut to control the flailing animal, the clock is stopped.

Bareback Riding

The aim of this event is to hang on to the bucking, twisting, sprinting bronco for eight seconds. As the animal rears out of its chute, the cowboy rides with his feet extended over the horse's shoulders. This first maneuver is called "marking out" (not to be confused with "making out"). As the horse bucks violently, the rider does his best to hold on—to a suitcase-type handle. Ride two-handed and you'll get a lower score. It's only a matter of seconds before the rider is thrown—but seconds count and the stakes are high.

Barrel Racing

A flat-out race to achieve the quickest time around three barrels positioned in a triangular shape. The horse is given a running start and can approach the course from either the left or right side. Riders face a five-second penalty if they knock over a barrel.

LEARN MORE

The PRCA (Professional Rodeo Cowboys Association) is the Pro Rodeo association and should be contacted for more information on the NFR or any other information on this fast and furious sport.
Find them at www.prorodeo.com.

Tie-down Roping

Formerly known as calf roping, this classic discipline is possibly among the most competitive of all the rodeo events. It's a contest for time and hard cash. Like the team roping event, the rider flies out from behind the barrier on horseback, this time chasing a calf. As he approaches the calf, he leaps from his horse and tackles the animal to the ground. With his rope, known as a *pigging string*, he ties three of the calf's legs securely. As soon as this is done, the clock is stopped.

Saddle Bronc Riding

The cowboy starts by "marking" his horse as he rides out of the chute. As the horse's front feet hit the ground the rider must have his spurs over the horse's shoulders. If not, he will be disqualified. Both horse and cowboy are judged by two judges each, aiming for the maximum of 100 points awarded (25 points per judge). The horse is judged by how hard it bucks and the cowboy is judged on control—notoriously difficult to maintain in this competition.

WORLD ICE GOLF CHAMPIONSHIPS

Polar bears can be ferocious, although they rarely pose a risk to humans. These incredibly strong animals have adapted to survive the harshest of environments where temperatures can fall to -60°F and icy plateaus stand between them and a good dinner. Such is the case in Northern Greenland, where in the depth of winter, the scenery is astoundingly beautiful. Pristine white terrain, majestic icebergs, and deep blue skies stretch impenetrably in all directions.

Comfortable in their frozen environs, the polar bears stroll with rhythm and grace, like lords surveying their manors. However, while their sense of smell is magnificent, they seem to ignore the scent of a very rare breed of animal that frequents these parts just once a year: the Ice Golfer.

Not far from the polar bears, a game of golf is going on in the vast expanse of ice into which a course has been sculpted. Clearly this is no ordinary game, as players brave the freezing temperatures to play a golf course like no other as they compete in The World Ice Golf Championships.

WORLD ICE GOLF CHAMPIONSHIPS
—THE BASIC FACTS

WHERE: The World Ice Golf Championships are held in Uummannaq, in North Western Greenland, 375 miles from the Polar Circle. Most of the population are Inuits, 2,700 of whom live in the district of Uummannaq.

WHEN: The championships have been running since 1997 and take place each year in March, although naturally, weather conditions can dictate when exactly the tournament is played.

THE COURSE: The course at Uummannaq is crafted from a frozen fjord just days before the main event. The layout of the course is governed by the climate, which creates a shift in the ice on a regular basis.

"It's the nearest thing to playing on the moon."
—Jack O'Keefe, U.S. 2004 runner-up

THE CLIMATE: Expect freezing cold temperatures for the few days you spend in Uummannaq, although the region experiences little snowfall. The beauty of the landscape is accentuated by piercing blue skies contrasting with the icy purity of the terrain. Temperatures range from -4°F to 14°F, so you can forget wearing your plus fours and polo shirts.

WHO: The championships are open to anyone with a handicap of 36 or under. To participate, make sure you've got the skill, the cash, and a very warm wardrobe. You'll be one of a maximum of 36 golfers who play the links.

HOW MUCH: Organizers charge approximately $5,000 per golfer to participate. Flights from Copenhagen to Uummannaq are included, as are full accommodations.

WORLD ICE GOLF CHAMPIONSHIPS
—IN MORE DETAIL

If you play the course at Uummannaq, you'll be one of the privileged few who have experienced arctic golf. Players have compared the scenery to Superman's home of Krypton, a seemingly other-worldly setting for an otherwise traditional game.

THE HISTORY

Ice golf is not a new phenomenon, although it's only in recent years that tournaments have been played in these harsher winter conditions. In the seventeenth century the game, known as *kolven,* was depicted by Dutch painter Aert van der Neer as being played on a frozen canal in Holland.

As equipment and clothing have improved to cater to subzero temperatures, so the game has developed and been promoted throughout the world. The championships in Uummannaq were devised by Arne Neimann, a hotel owner from the area. In 1997, he commissioned the first course and—together with the local community, Uummannaq Municipality, and Greenland Tourism—the World Ice Golf Champion-ships were born. Now, in addition to

providing golfers with an experience that will stay with them throughout their lives, it provides a valuable source of income for the local Inuit community.

THE COURSE

The course is one of rare beauty. Framed by icebergs and glaciers, it meanders through snowdrifts and layers of ice formed over thousands of years. This is a dynamic course, with the links changing shape as the ice shifts beneath it, some-times before your very eyes. If high winds blow, they create ridges and compressions on the surface. Tee off as soon as you can before new obsta-cles develop. Wait too long in harsher condi-tions and you could find yourself faced with an arctic bunker settling in halfway down the fairway.

It's a nine-hole, 36-par course, with two rounds of nine holes played on each of

the two days of the championships. The course ideally consists of 5 par 4s, 2 par 3s, and 2 par 5s, with the format governed by ice formations and the unpredictable topography.

Playing each hole requires adapting your technique to its rough and uneven surfaces, which frequently have a ½-to-1-inch covering of frozen powder. The rules do, however, allow you to smooth the area around the ball before your shot.

THE EQUIPMENT

Not surprisingly, a traditional white golf ball won't help your game. A fluorescent orange ball is used instead, so you can actually see it.

The organizers recommend bringing a half set of clubs to the event (3, 5, 7, 9, PW, SW, as well as a 3 or 5 wood). Use steel shafted clubs as these offer more resistance against the freezing temperatures and when playing on difficult, harder terrain. However, to avoid the need to have them surgically removed, make sure you're wearing gloves when taking your shots—and not just the thin golf gloves, either.

With the arctic temperatures you'll need to be on the move constantly, so the ban on carts and caddies works in your favor. Warm clothing is clearly essential; professionals recommend a layering effect to allow you to swing comfortably and shed a layer when necessary. Wear a warm pair of boots, and remember your sunglasses and a high SPF sun block.

SOME GOOD ADVICE

Polar explorer Pen Hadow, who has close ties with the championships, has some good advice for ice golfers.

1. When striking the ball, remember that due to air pressure, the ball will only travel 80 percent of the distance it would travel in normal conditions. Drive low and hard and allow the ball to bounce to cover the required distance.

2. Although playing conditions are safe and officials surround the course, when playing around the edge of the fjord, keep an eye on any holes in the ice. These are breathing holes created by seals. While seals are gracious creatures, one thing's for sure, they won't be returning your ball.

3. It's very rare for a human to be attacked by a polar bear, but if you come face to face with one, don't run away. Always remember that polar bears can run faster than humans and if they see you running, you'll be considered as prey. If you are attacked, curl up in the fetal position with your arms over your head.

Finally, as a rookie, don't let the ice golfing veterans talk you into exchanging your sand wedge for a snow wedge. A snow wedge is what arctic explorers use to wipe their backsides.

LEARN MORE

To inquire about competing, contact:

World Ice Golf Committee, Greenland
P.O. Box 202
DK-3961 Uummannaq
Greenland

SOCCER AT BARCELONA'S CAMP NOU

"Barcelona versus Real Madrid is the only fixture in the world that can draw so many fans twice a year, every year. Throw into the equation all the history, all the media attention and you are looking at a powder keg."

— Bobby Robson, former F.C. Barcelona coach

For the Spanish, the big soccer game (what the rest of the world calls "football") of the season is undoubtedly Barcelona versus Real Madrid. And the best place to watch it? Camp Nou (Our Stadium), home to F.C. Barcelona, or El Barça. Unless, of course, you're a Real Madrid fan.

This is turf war on a large scale. Tension builds weeks in advance of the big game and, for some, from the start of the soccer season. For Catalans, F.C. Barcelona is much more than a club. It's a symbol of their fierce regional pride. And when that pride is threatened by their archrival Real Madrid, they take it very seriously indeed.

SOCCER AT BARCELONA'S CAMP NOU
— THE BASIC FACTS

WHEN: It's the national soccer event. To be part of it, you'll need to check out the Spanish soccer season schedule (what they call "fixtures") on the team Web site to get the latest dates for the Barça versus Real Madrid match.

WHERE: Barcelona is one of Europe's most progressive capitals, with strong traditions and a vibrant and modern cultural scene. It is the capital of the province of Catalunya and is situated on the northeast coast of Spain.

THE STADIUM: Built in 1957, Camp Nou is a monster of a stadium and a provincial landmark. At 157 feet high and with a surface area of 180,445 square feet, the stadium can seat 100,000 spectators and in an emergency can be evacuated in five minutes.

WHAT: This is soccer's biggest matchup (or derby) when the two rival teams, Barcelona and Real Madrid, face each other to uphold the honor of their countrymen. And, of course, win a soccer match.

HOW: Getting in to see this great game at Camp Nou will be tough, but greatly rewarded. Make sure you book your tickets well in advance. Try buying them from the ticket booths in the city center called *taquilla*, or book online before you travel.

HOW MUCH: Normal tickets will cost between $20 and $50, but be prepared to pay a lot more for the big match.

HOW TO GET THERE: If you find yourself in a cab with a driver who doesn't know where Camp Nou is, he's either from Madrid or he really is taking you for a ride. You can also reach Camp Nou on the underground subway system. Travel to either Collblanc station on blue Line 5 or Maria Cristina station on green Line 3.

SOCCER AT BARCELONA'S CAMP NOU
—IN MORE DETAIL

If you're in the stands at Camp Nou for this matchup, you're in for an amazing experience. The Barça fans vastly outnumber the visiting Real Madrid fans, often by as much as 30 to one. With a capacity of 100,000 fans, that's a lot of noise and a sea of red and blue rocking to the Barça rhythms and chants. Colored smoke fills the air, fireworks sear from the stands into the sky above, and the crowd erupts as the players run onto the field.

Despite a slightly more subdued encounter in April 2004, the animosity between the two clubs can be acutely felt by the players on the field, especially those who decide to defect from Barcelona to Real Madrid. During the 2002 game, a glass whisky bottle and coins were thrown at Luis Figo as he went to take Real Madrid's first corner of the match. Figo was being punished for what the Barça fans saw as a betrayal. Some newspapers reported a pig's head being thrown at his feet. Missiles aside, on match day the atmosphere is one not to be missed. It's the ultimate showdown and as much a political wrangle as a sporting one.

A HISTORY OF CONFLICT

The aggression between the two clubs has developed over decades of disharmony and distrust. This is not about soccer, but rather a feud formed in history. During the Spanish Civil War (1936–39), Catalunya rebelled against Franco's rule and as a consequence was persecuted during his regime. Camp Nou became a symbol of freedom of speech and Catalan spirit—a sanctuary where Catalans could protest their sense of injustice and voice their opinions. Add to that the fact that Franco was a Real Madrid fan, and the reasons for this enmity become even more apparent.

CLUB HISTORY—REAL MADRID

Real Madrid was founded by a group of soccer fans in 1902. On May 13, 1902, the first match between Real Madrid and Barcelona was held. Barcelona won 3—1. However, in 1902 it was Real Madrid who lifted the first trophy of their history, the Copa de la Gran Peña.

In 1905, Real Madrid won its first Spanish Championship, beating Athlétic Bilbao 1—0. In the early 1940s, Santiago Bernabéu became a vitally important figure in Real Madrid's history. He was elected president in 1943 and planned grand projects to secure the future of Real Madrid as one of the world's greatest teams. Bernabéu even wielded a pick on the first day of the building of the new Real Madrid stadium.

Sixty years of soccer achievement followed, and in 2002 Real Madrid celebrated its centenary year. Suitably, in this celebratory year, they became European Champions for the ninth time by defeating Bayer Leverkussen 2—1. Today, they boast one of the most internationally acclaimed teams in the world with high caliber players and celebrities such as David Beckham, Zinedine Zidane, and Luis Figo.

CLUB HISTORY—F.C. BARCELONA

In Europe, Barcelona has often played in the shadows of their archrival Real Madrid. It is still, however, the most supported club in the world.

Founded in 1899 by Hans Gamper, F.C. Barcelona has an illustrious history of cup wins and championship victories. With similar grand-scale stadium ambitions as Real Madrid, Camp Nou was built to house its devout Catalan fans and was extended for the Spanish World Cup in 1982.

One of the club's great achievements is to have qualified and played in every European Cup since 1955. In Barça's centenary year, 1999, it won the national championship for the sixteenth time, thus adding to the celebrations.

Camp Nou continues to be home to great players and heroes. Johann Cruyff, Diego Maradona, Romario, and Ronaldo all have places in the club's history.

HOW DO THEY COMPARE?

Real Madrid Silverware

Spanish Champions: 29 times
Copa Del Rey Champions: 17 times
Super Copa Champions: 5 times
European Champions Cup Winners: 8 times
UEFA Cup Champions: 2 times

F.C. Barcelona Silverware

Spanish Champions: 16 times
Copa Del Rey Champions: 24 times
Super Copa Champions: 9 times
European Champions Cup winners: 1 time
UEFA Cup Champions: 3 times

LEARN MORE
To find out more, check out the official club sites:
www.fcbarcelona.com
www.realmadrid.com

London, SW19, rain, umbrellas, Cliff Richard, straw-berries and cream, and great British optimism. All synonymous with one immense sporting spectacle: tennis at Wimbledon.

Wimbledon is an event that generally cheers up a nation. It signals the start of the British summer and it stirs a nationalistic pride that seldom surfaces on such a grand scale. It's an international tournament of grand repute—the one everyone wants to win, and winning it becomes the pinnacle of a player's career.

Wimbledon is a high point in every country's sport-ing calendar as they cheer on their respective tennis stars. Some local heroes, perhaps internationally unknown, dream of annihilating the top seeds and usurping the great kings and queens of the game. And the exciting thing about Wimbledon is, exactly that can happen.

WIMBLEDON—THE BASIC FACTS

WHAT: The greatest tennis tournament of them all. Wimbledon holds a prestige with which no other championship comes near to competing. Its sense of tradition and identity is anchored in 130 years of history.

WHERE: Wimbledon, Greater London, SW19. Just down the hill from the exclusive Wimbledon Village, which is hijacked by tennis stars for the two weeks of the tournament.

WHEN: The last week of June and first week of July.

WHO: Anyone who's anyone competes at Wimbledon. The big guns have their profiles and reputations to uphold, and the novices have great ambitions to un-leash their potential in front of the savvy Wimbledon crowds and potential big-brand sponsors.

HOW MANY: The Wimbledon seating capacity is 35,000. In 2003, more than 470,000 spectators filled the stands over the two weeks of the tournament. As it was broadcast in 164 countries, an additional 1.8 billion people had television exposure to the event.

HOW MUCH: Week one tickets are distributed to the public via a lottery system. If your name's not on the list then you may get lucky in the second week. Week two tickets sold at the gates can range from about $30 to $120. They'll be hard to come by, however, as this is one event that's guaranteed to be sold out.

HOW TO GET IN: If you're paying a spontaneous visit to Wimbledon in the second week of the tourna-ment, be prepared to stand in line, preferably at the front, as there are often only a limited number sold at the gate. If you're really passion-ate about getting into Center Court, bring your tent, a sleeping bag, and long johns to settle in for the night. Be warned, it gets cold out there.

HOW TO GET THERE: The courts of the All England Lawn Tennis & Croquet Club are easily accessible with shuttle services organized for the tourna-ment's two weeks. There are regular trains from London Waterloo to Wimbledon. The District Line underground service will also take you to South-fields, where it's a short walk to the most famous courts in history.

It's a gloriously sunny day and, because Wimbledon is so often blighted by downpours, everyone is making the most of it. Office productivity rates plummet as workers catch the match on TV or log on to the Internet for live scores. Inside the Wimbledon gates, crowds gather to watch the big screen on Henman Hill. The baskets of strawberries and cream are rapidly selling out and the Pimms is flowing. On Center Court, the tension is palpable as a great British hope battles his way into the quarterfinals.

THE HISTORY

The All England Croquet Club was founded in 1868. It wasn't until 1875 that lawn tennis was added to the club's activities. The game was introduced by Major Walter Wingfield who, influenced by Royal Tennis (particularly popular with Henry VIII in sixteenth century England)

and other racquet games, devised a new game called *Sphairistiké*.

By the spring of 1877, croquet was taking second billing to the increasingly popular lawn tennis and the club became known as the All England Lawn Tennis & Croquet Club. It held its first Lawn Tennis Championship that same year.

At the beginning of the 20th century, lawn tennis had an international appeal. The American contingent was strong, although the introduction of the game to the United States was relatively recent (in 1874, by Mary Ewing Outerbridge of New York). In 1905, May Sutton did the U.S. proud and became the first overseas champion to win the Ladies Singles.

In 1922, the All England Club moved to its current address where a seating capacity of 14,000 dramatically increased the appeal of the game. As air travel became more prevalent, from the 1950s onwards, Wimbledon became the favored destination for the modern, affluent tennis fan. Its appeal to the broader public developed

with increased television coverage, and by 1968, with the help of such talented champions as Billie Jean King and Rod Laver, Wimbledon had truly achieved its status as the premier tennis championship. It's a big money event, too, with prize money in 2003 standing at about $1.1 million for the Men's Champion and about $1 million for the Ladies' Champion. But it's the Wimbledon title that's the real motivation for the players.

THE BIG NAMES

Over its rich history, Wimbledon has seen some incredible champions and has provided some great sporting moments, from John McEnroe's racquet-flinging antics and verbal outbursts to Serena Williams' powerful serves and

risque fashions. And who can forget the fascinating finals of 2001, with Goran Ivanisevic's victory over Pat Rafter? Watching pain turn to elation on the faces of winners is a sight that Center Court crowds pay a lot of money to enjoy.

Among many others, Wimbledon has hosted such sporting giants as Bjorn Borg, Pete Sampras, Arthur Ashe, Boris Becker, and Fred Perry. And there are the legendary Martina Navratilova, Venus and Serena Williams, and Chris Evert. And there's always an abundance of new talent on the tennis circuit waiting for their names to be etched on the silverware.

The $64,000 question: will the Brits, hosts to this glorious competition, ever see another golden era like that of 1934 to 1937, when a total of 11 titles were won, including three singles in succession by the great Fred Perry? Wimbledon's host country hopes it's only a matter of time.

LEARN MORE

Visit www.wimbledon.org to relive history or to find out the latest on the Championships.

SEA POWER

ACAPULCO CLIFF DIVING

Diving in Acapulco is like throwing yourself head first off the edge of the world. It takes the bravest of men to climb the cliffs at La Quebrada and then plunge themselves into the crashing waves below, risking their lives and putting on a spectacular show.

For the men, it's not just their lives they're worried about but also what's tucked inside their Speedos. Hitting the water at incredible speed, the Acapulco cliff dive is a true test of manhood, in more ways than one. It's only the bravest of divers who takes on the world's greatest head-first challenge. Of course women who take the plunge won't face the same problem, but need the same nerves of steel and perfect technique to steer them away from the rocks below.

ACAPULCO CLIFF DIVING—THE BASIC FACTS

WHERE: Acapulco, in South Mexico, has a population of more than 700,000. La Quebrada, a jagged rock formation on Acapulco's Pacific coast, provides a dramatic setting for cliff diving spectacles.

WHEN: This region of Mexico boasts 360 days of sunshine each year. So you'll most likely have beautiful blue skies under which, five times a day every day, you can watch the diving. Starting at 1:00 p.m. the performances run as late as 10:30 at night. After dark the divers climb the rock bearing torches, which then illuminate their flight from the cliff top.

WHO: Only the most experienced of divers should even contemplate the plunge from La Quebrada. It is a perilous leap of faith. Unless you have experience, technique, a head for heights, and—importantly—permission, stick to watching.

HOW HIGH: 148 feet, the equivalent of a 15-story building.

HOW FAST: At the moment of impact, divers have reached speeds up to 80 mph. The spectacle is over within the blink of an eye and the seconds after the dive are fraught with anxiety, the crowds willing the diver to resurface unscathed.

HOW TO GET THERE: Acapulco's Alvarez International Airport will be your main access to the city, particularly good for flights to and from the United States, Canada, and Europe. Once in town, the cliffs can be reached on foot from Calle La Quebrada or by taxi.

WHERE TO WATCH FROM: People have been watching the diving from Plaza Las Glorias El Mirador Hotel for many years. It's here that you get an excellent view of the divers and their descent into the deep blue waters below.

Cliff diving is part of Acapulco's lifeblood and of iconic importance. It is both a local and tourist attraction, with divers coming mainly from the vicinity.

The climb to the top of La Quebrada is grueling, but once there the view is incredible. Peering over the edge, the drop is alarmingly severe, especially if you're about to hurl yourself over it. The waves pummel the rocks and the powerful ocean, like a hungry, slavering wolf eyeing its prey, demonstrates its eagerness to swallow you up whole.

THE DIVERS

While many international diving competitions have been held in Acapulco, including the World Cliff Diving Championships, only a few big international names have made the dive, despite the fact that there are several hundred registered high divers. For many of them, the risk is just too great.

In the sport of high diving, athletes are invited to compete by merit of their reputation and the records they have achieved. One such diver who made the headlines by becoming one of the first five women to accomplish the feat was Montana Miller, a student from Harvard University. In November, 1996, she made history:

"As she emerges from the sea, Miller will be among the first women allowed to join the elite of Acapulco cliff divers, who for more than six decades have awed tourists—and later, international television audiences—with daredevil feats from one of the most dramatic settings of the high-diving world."

—The Washington Post

THE TECHNIQUE

Acapulco divers are true athletes. They are supple, flexible, and elastic—and they need to be, as their jump requires precision in order to avoid an almost certain death. The skill factor for an Acapulco dive is much higher than that of any of its nearest competitors. Divers must dive out horizontally approximately 30 feet in order to end up in the ocean rather than flattened on the rocks below. Their point of entry is within an inlet just 22 feet wide with water barely 13 feet deep.

Entering the sea at speeds of up to 80 mph means technique and timing must be perfect. Get it wrong and you'll experience a brand new type of pain. Hitting a piece of seaweed or a fish can result in a broken foot (one of the most common injuries). Land on your backside too often and you'll gain a reputation as an "enema diver."

Added to this, in Acapulco, timing your entry into the water can mean the difference between life and death. Assessing the ebb and flow of the waves beneath you

LEARN MORE

The obvious way to find out more is to actually go there. Give the divers a tip to show your appreciation of their performance, and listen to their tales of scrapes with death. If you're lucky they'll show you their scars.

To hone your knowledge have a chat with the Mexican tourist board. You can find more details about Acapulco at www.visitmexico.com.

is imperative, as they cushion your landing and their currents draw you away from the sharp rocks beneath the surface.

GOOD OLD-FASHIONED ADVICE

One of today's great high divers who has made the dive in Acapulco, Dustin Webster, has three rules that should be heeded by anyone who intends to master the sport while staying in one piece:

1. Always check out the dive site for yourself. Take your mask and snorkel and make sure you're not at risk of impaling yourself on rocks.

2. Keep your entry spot in your mind at all times. Never lose sight of the point at which you need to enter the water.
3. Keep your legs together, unless you have an ambition to sing falsetto in the local choir.

THE HISTORY

The tradition of cliff diving in Acapulco started in 1934 as a test of bravado between friends. It quickly began to attract an audience and is now a tradition passed down through the generations. The dive is practiced from an early age at heights of 100 feet, and it's not uncommon to see young boys diving from the lower cliffs as their fathers twist and somersault from the dizzying heights above. These experienced, local divers are known as the *Clavadistas*.

Raul Garcia Bravo, the most famous veteran of the local *Club de Clavadistas*, Club of High Divers, claims to have made an incredible 37,000 dives.

THE AMERICA'S CUP

If, when asked about sailors, your mind immediately conjures up thoughts of old salts with barnacle-encrusted white beards, pipes, and holey sweaters, then you need our help.

Brand-name waterproof clothing, ultra-cool sunglasses and bank vaults full of cash are definitely *de rigueur* when it comes to the America's Cup, the most prestigious boat race in the world.

You'll need to shell out some big money to take part in this race, so it's no surprise that teams are bankrolled by fat-cat industry leaders and heavyweight corporate sponsors. Investment is crucial to ensure the most experienced crew and the most advanced hardware to secure the best chance of winning the 32nd America's Cup.

THE AMERICA'S CUP—THE BASIC FACTS

WHEN: The 32nd America's Cup takes place in 2007. That's not to say time stands still in the yachting world until then. Far from it, the action starts in 2004 and continues until 2007. Each "act" of the America's Cup (which comprises a series of races) is held in a different location around the world.

WHERE: In 2007, for the first time in 152 years, the America's Cup will be held in Europe. Valencia, Spain, will host events in 2004 and the final in 2007. Regattas will also be held in the United States in 2005.

WHAT: The America's Cup comprises two core competitions. The first, the Louis Vuitton Cup, pits the main challengers against each other to decide which one will oppose the defender of the America's Cup.

WHO: This is a sport for the serious seafarer. Teams, known as syndicates, spend big money to select experienced professionals to help mount a challenge. There are often over 100 people involved in coordinating one team's challenge with the backing of powerful corporate sponsors.

HOW MUCH: Unless you have a very wealthy owner, your team will need sponsorship to raise the $60 to $80 million needed to mount a challenge. If you've got your act together, you'll be courted by some big corporate sponsors. Some of the smaller, newer syndicates have devised imaginative marketing tactics. The U.S. Sausalito Challenge syndicate, for example, held an auction on eBay to auction its sponsorship and marketing rights.

THE AMERICA'S CUP—IN MORE DETAIL

THE HISTORY

In 1851, the Brits were defeated by America in a "friendly" race around the Isle of Wight. The silver cup given to the New York Yacht Club became known as the America's Cup. A trust deed (known as the "Deed of Gift") established the rules of competition between countries. It encourages the club holding the cup to reach agreement with challengers on how the race is organized. The protocol defines the set of challenges to be undertaken within the competition to choose a challenger of the defender. If an agreement cannot be reached, the Deed of Gift will specify the competition conditions.

THE LOUIS VUITTON CUP FORMAT

The organizers of the America's Cup equate this prestigious event to a story unfolding in a play. The acts are held in numerous locations from 2004 to 2006, with the final act played out by the challenger and defender in Valencia in 2007.

The Louis Vuitton Cup starts with a round robin, in which each challenger races each of the others once per round. This first tournament seeds the best teams from one to eight.

The Louis Vuitton Quarters then splits the eight into two, with the stronger contenders (seeds one to four) placed in a "Double Chance" group and the weaker (seeds five to eight) in a "Single Chance" group. The top ranked in each group are allowed to choose their opponents. The quarters see the elimination of the last two "Single Chance" teams and qualification for the semifinals for the top two "Double Chance" teams.

The quarterfinals Repechage allows the two "Double Chance" losers to take their second opportunity against the winning "Single Chances." The winners from the Double and Single Chances pairs will make up the third and fourth places in the semifinals. The two losers are eliminated.

And so we're down to four. The Double Chance crews race each other. The Single Chance crews race against each other and, as before, the loser is eliminated. Three teams are still in the competition.

The winner of the Single Chance race must then face the loser of the Double Chance race to decide who goes into the final Cup round.

With two teams now left, the Challenger Showdown finally eliminates one and selects the winner, who challenges the Defender of the America's Cup.

And then there were two, Challenger and Defender, ready for the duel they've been dreaming of for so long. And they know that in this race, there is no second place.

THE TEAM

Each team is run as a business with investors and suppliers. The larger team may comprise a hundred people, from yacht designers to sail makers, nautical engineers to accountants. However, it's the 16 skilled sailors who make up the crew, along with one owner's representative who must have no part to play in the racing of the yacht.

The winning team of 2003 was the yacht *Alinghi*, an international team based in Switzerland. It represents the Société Nautique de Genève, and its success has brought the America's Cup to Europe for the first time in 152 years.

LEARN MORE

Want to know more? Keep up with the action by visiting the official site at www.americascup.com.

FINDING YOUR WAY AROUND A YACHT

"When you spend so much time pushing, caring for, cajoling, and maintaining a beautiful racing machine like this, you get very close. She's looked after me well, and I look after her. I haven't been lonely at all."

—Ellen MacArthur, who sailed around the world single-handed in her boat *Kingfisher*

BOW: This is the bowman and mid-bowman's territory. It's where the headsails are set and the spinnaker pole changed from side to side. There are no guardrails on an America's Cup boat so the bowman must have great agility, boat skills, resilience, and courage to work on the bow, the most exposed and unstable part of the boat.

DECK LAYOUT: There is no cabin or area down below. The deck is a functional place, organized so that the 16 crew members can perform their roles with maximum efficiency. Heavy loads mean that nothing can be controlled without a winch. There are 12 winches in total. The twin steering wheels are connected to the rudder and trim tab, a flap on the back of the keel, which control the boat's direction.

HULL: The boat is 80 feet long and its dimensions must conform to those set out by the America's Cup Class Rule. The hull is built in a mold using materials such as carbon, kevlar, titanium, glass fiber, aluminum, and steel.

KEEL: A large fin attached to a lead-filled bulb, the keel stops the boat from capsizing and counteracts the pressure made on the sails by the wind. It weighs about 20 tons and represents 80 percent of the entire boat's weight. Each boat's keel design is one of the America's Cup's most closely guarded secrets.

MAST AND BOOM (KNOWN JOINTLY AS THE RIG): The mast is the vertical spar, made of carbon fiber, up which the mainsail and various headsails are hoisted. It is about 110 feet tall and weighs 1,750 pounds. The boom, a carbon fiber spar about 30 feet long, supports the foot of the mainsail. It weighs about 150 pounds.

SAILS: There are three main types of sail used on an America's Cup boat: a mainsail, headsail (jib), and spinnaker, the huge, colorful sail flown at the front when sailing downwind.

STERN: The rear part of the boat.

"Not tragic to die doing what you love. You want the ultimate thrill, you gotta be willing to pay the ultimate price."

—Bodhi, *Point Break*, 1991, director Kathryn Bigelow

Giant, storm-brewed waves swell and crash to shore. Never will an amateur ingest so much salt water and risk so much pain than when facing the awesome power of the North Shore waves off Oahu's Pacific coast. The ocean is imposing and threatening, and its monster rollers dwarf any human life form that endeavors to conquer them. That's why, in Hawaii's winter months, these beasts are left to the pros.

Hawaii has a natural birthright when it comes to staging the world's greatest surfing events. Its royal ancestors invented this great sport. Its beaches provide the ultimate surfing challenges to the most experienced of riders, with the North Shore coral reefs providing the perfect conditions for men and women to master their trade.

THE VANS TRIPLE CROWN OF SURFING —THE BASIC FACTS

The Vans Triple Crown of Surfing is the event that all the pros want to compete in, and win—if they're good enough. The waves are huge, the competition is fierce, and the prize money's pretty much the best there is. This championship is comparable to the Super Bowl, and for surfing participants and fans there's no other place on earth to get such a massive, natural high.

WHERE: Oahu is Hawaii's most populated island with more than 800,000 inhabitants. With lush rainforests and more than 20 miles of sandy beaches, it is also an island of great natural diversity. Add to this a climate where the average daily temperature is 84°F, and Oahu becomes a very attractive tourist destination, particularly if you own a board.

MEN'S EVENTS: The Triple Crown is staged at three renowned big-wave locations on Hawaii's North Shore: Haleiwa, Sunset Beach, and Bells Beach. The competition builds to a grand finale at Bells Beach, home to the Banzai Pipeline.
Haleiwa: Hawaiian Pro
Sunset Beach: Rip Curl Cup
Bells Beach: Rip Curl Pipeline Masters

WOMEN'S EVENTS: For the women's Triple Crown, two events are hosted on the North Shore and a third in Maui:
Haleiwa: The Roxy Pro
Turtle Bay Resort: Women's Pro
Honolua Bay, Maui: Billabong Pro

WHAT: Surfers are competing for world titles, Vans Triple Crown of Surfing titles, and qualification for the following year's events.

HOW HIGH: The biggest waves in the winter season can reach 30 feet in height. That's the equivalent of a four-story building.

WHEN: The Triple Crown takes place from mid-November to the end of December every year, starting with the Hawaiian Pro contest in November. You'll catch the waves in their prime in these winter months, but to ride them confidently you'll need to have spent more than a few hours boogie boarding on your vacation.

WHO: The world's greatest professional surfers take part in the Vans Triple Crown of Surfing. Champions such as Myles Padaca and brothers Andy and Bruce Irons battle with the elements to secure the prestigious titles.

HOW TO GET THERE: To reach Oahu, you'll fly to the island's main city, Honolulu. Take a bus or a car to reach the North Shore. The island is small and a special bus service can take you around it in as little as four hours.

THE VANS SURFING TRIPLE CROWN
—IN MORE DETAIL

Winter in Hawaii is a perfect time to experience the beauty, majesty, and raw adrenaline of surfing. To many it's a way of life, a passion, and an addiction. Once in their blood, mastering the skill to harness the ocean's powers becomes an irresistible challenge. Many writers have praised those who risk their lives to master their craft:

"Where but the moment before was only the wide desolation and invincible roar, is now a man, erect, full statured, not-struggling frantically in that wild movement, not buried and crushed and buffeted by those mighty monsters, but standing above them all, calm and superb, poised on the giddy summit, his feet buried in the churning foam, the salt smoke rising to his knees, and all the rest of him in the free air and flashing sunlight, and he is flying through the air, flying forward, flying fast as the surge on which he stands. He is a Mercury—a brown Mercury. His heels are winged, and in them is the swiftness of the sea."

—Jack London, 1907,
"A Royal Sport: Surfing in Waikiki"

SURFING HISTORY

Historians have gleaned much of surfing's ancient past through drawings carved into Hawaii's rocks. Called *He'enalu*, or "wave sliding," it was the sport of the Polynesian kings who ruled the Hawaiian islands more than 2,000 years ago. Through He'enalu, they maintained their strength, stamina, and agility.

The earliest written records of the sport can be found in 1789 journal entries of the island's first Western visitors. Not long after this, and despite its long history, surfing became almost extinct on the island as missionaries condemned its widespread practice, denouncing it as a hedonistic pursuit.

In 1907, Jack London, already an acclaimed writer of books that found their inspiration in nature, came to Hawaii. His discovery of the sport and the skills of its practitioners led to a revival. He wrote of George Freeth, who earned the title "the first man to surf California" by surfing the West Coast in spectacular style. Freeth also revolutionized surfing by reducing the redwood and balsa wood board to half the size of its predecessors and, as a result, devising new techniques to ride the waves.

In 1912, a young Hawaiian boy called Duke Paoa Kahanamoku was hanging out with friends in Waikiki. Known as the "Beach boys of Waikiki," Duke and his friends further helped to resuscitate the royal sport. Duke competed in the 1920 and 1924 Olympics and starred in many Hollywood movies. With every opportunity he promoted surfing to an engrossed public. In the 1950s and '60s the sport was fast

becoming a global phenomenon, thanks to music from the Beach Boys and the young and fashionable California beach scene. On today's circuit, surfing competitions are held throughout the world in Hawaii, Australia, Tahiti, Fiji, South Africa, Japan, California, France, the United Kingdom, Spain, and Brazil.

THE TRIPLE CROWN MEN'S EVENTS

The men's events are closely contested each year, with the major titles fought for by the best names in surfing. The Vans Triple Crown of Surfing is a big event in the surfing calendar, with the prize purse

at an impressive $750,000, and with first prizes of up to $30,000.

Hawaiian Pro, the first of the three competitions, takes place in early to mid-November. The ride is fast onto a coral reef near the shore and surfers take the opportunity to get in some creative moves.

The Rip Curl Cup at Sunset Beach is held in late November to early December. This competition requires a different technique, with big waves swelling and breaking half a mile out to sea in extremely deep water.

The culmination of the Vans Triple Crown of Surfing happens in December, with the Banzai Pipeline, the focal point of the Pipeline Masters. This is one of the most spectacular surfing shows on the planet, as the pipeline combines both speed and power to demand the very best performance from those who ride it. Held only 100 feet from shore, this is both dangerous and awe-inspiring as competitors seemingly glide effortlessly through the barrel of the wave before dipping out to skim the surfaces above a barely submerged coral reef.

The Pipeline Masters, begun in 1970, is the longest running professional surfing competition.

RULES AND ADVICE

It's always good to have a surf partner, a "brah," the kind of bud who'll spur you on when you've fallen off your board 50 times in one day. You'll keep an eye out for each other and experience each other's successes, quickly forgetting the failures.

Before you take to your board, watch what others are doing and learn from their mistakes. Take note of where the waves are breaking and where people are paddling out to. If you're inexperienced, make sure you practice on a sandy beach where the waves aren't going to rise to 20 feet, take you by the scruff of the neck, and dump you on the coral below.

There aren't too many rules in surfing. You just need to obey the golden ones set out below. If you don't, you'll know about it, as "getting killed" is often a punishment from other surfers for those who stray (it's more of a fist in the face than a mortal blow).

Wave Ownership (The My Wave Rule)

The surfer closest to the breaking point of the wave has the right of way. However, if you're paddling into the wave and someone is already riding it, you do not have the right to own the wave.

Dropping In (The Shalt Not Rule)

Never, ever, drop in—that is, to set off on a wave in front of someone who is already riding it. You definitely won't be thanked.

Paddling Out (The Eat It Rule)

Stay behind the surfer who's already riding the wave. You may lose your opportunity to pick up a wave, but another will come along.

THE EQUIPMENT

Some might tell you that the most essential piece of kit a surfer can possess is a 1960s VW micro bus. Not true. Your bus won't help you become a god on the waves. This is the real stuff you need:

The Board—If you're a novice, buy it second hand. Don't spend your hard-earned cash on a new one until you can stand up on your bargain basement board. Better to let the hand-me-down take all the punishment a learner inflicts on it.

A Leash—This connects you to your board. The leash will save you having to swim out to face the brother of the wave that just wiped you out.

Sunblock—It takes a good few years to build up a professional tan. If you're fair skinned, it might never happen. So be safe and take a high SPF sunblock because you may well be waiting all day for the perfect wave.

TALKING LIKE A PRO

You may have the sun-bleached, long blond hair, sun-kissed skin, and the coolest gear, but you also need to speak the lingo. The surfer's vernacular changes all the time, and if you're new to the sport and hanging out on Waikiki Beach, you'll hear some unfamiliar terms. This list is definitely not exhaustive, but will give you some words to convince your friends that you've really *Been There, Done That*.

Describing Waves

- Barrel—hollow *tube* between the throwing *lip* and the face of the wave
- Tube—see *barrel*
- Lip—the crest of a wave, which spills down over the face to create a *tube*
- Beach break—waves breaking close to

the beach or on a sandbank

- Confused—small to medium waves that are too choppy to surf with style
- Epic—really great waves
- Gnarly—big, powerful waves that challenge even the greatest surfers
- Phat wave—a beautiful wave to ride

Surfing Technique

- Backhand surfing—riding with your back to the wave
- Backdoor—Taking off behind the peak on a hollow wave
- El Rollo—Rolling 360° with the *lip* of the wave
- Stevie Wonder—performing with your eyes closed
- Rip—surf with great technique and style
- Goofy foot—surfing with your right foot forward
- Drop in—when a surfer catches a wave and drops to the bottom. See Rules and Advice above.

Other People

- Da' bomb—an amazing boarder
- Basil—a very cool body boarder
- Turon—a tourist who has little clue what they're doing
- Mahoo—a very derogatory term for a surfer with no style

X **Place your picture here**

LEARN MORE

To get the latest competition results and find out more information on the biggest events, visit www.triplecrownofsurfing.com.

- Resin monkey—again, a derogatory term for stand-up surfers
- Gremos—no cluers
- Grommet—a young novice

Wipe Out Terms

- Blasted
- Bullwinkled
- Drilled—particularly when you wipe out and hit the bottom or rocks
- Worked—being beaten up by a wave
- Nailed

General

- Aloha!—general informal greeting to your buddies
- Ate it—he/she bit the dust
- Killa warra—an expression of delight
- Bra (h)— surfing partner, your best buddy
- Beef—your board
- Lube—board wax

THE MONACO GRAND PRIX
—JEWEL OF FORMULA ONE

How's this for a dream: You've won the Monaco Grand Prix, and on your victory lap you wave to the scantily clad beauties hanging from balconies above the track. And for once, they're waving back at you. On the podium you spray champagne over the two losers and later mingle with the glitterati at the evening's dinner held in your honor. Go on, shake your fist angrily: This is what you were born for, not logging mindless hours in a cubicle prison.

This is truly the stuff of dreams: the glamour, the opulence, the speed, and the smell of burning rubber. On race weekend, the Mediterranean is studded with cruisers and yachts and the light is intense and omnipresent, piercing the deep blue sky, reflected in Ray Bans, and bouncing whimsically off the jewelry of the rich and famous.

One of the greatest vantage points for watching the Monaco Grand Prix is your TV set, from the comfort of your armchair . . . which is lucky because that's exactly where you probably are. However, it's only when you're in Monaco that you really understand why this race is hailed as the veritable king of the auto racing calendar.

THE MONACO GRAND PRIX—THE BASIC FACTS
THE FORMULA ONE SEASON: March to October.

NUMBER OF CIRCUITS VISITED IN A SEASON: Eighteen.

MONACO GRAND PRIX LAP DISTANCE: 3.4 kilometers (approximately 2 miles). The only street race in the Formula One calendar.

THE RACE: 263 kilometers (approximately 164 miles) over 78 laps.

PARTICIPANTS: 10 constructors, each with two drivers; only those who qualify within the allocated time will compete in the race.

FIRST MONACO GRAND PRIX: April 14, 1929.

RACE ORGANIZER: Automobile Club de Monaco. Their president, Anthony Noghes, and renowned Monegasque racing driver, Louis Chiron, proposed the street race to Prince Louis II in the mid-1920s.

DRIVERS WITH MOST WINS AT MONACO: Ayrton Senna: 6 wins; Michael Schmuacher: 5 wins.

WINNER'S TIME IN 2004: Jarno Trulli, Grand Prix winner in 2004 finished in one hour, 45 minutes, 46 seconds in his Renault.

FASTEST LAP TIME IN 2004: Michael Schumacher, Ferrari, in one minute, 14 seconds.

THE STAGE IS SET

The setting for the Monaco Grand Prix is spectacular. Situated between the Alps and the Mediterranean, Monaco also lies between the Italian and the French Rivieras. No wonder this rich man's playground attracts so many visitors every year. Here are the facts:

• The Principality of Monaco is just over 3 miles long and under 0.6 mile wide.
• It's the second smallest independent state in the world (after Vatican City).
• It has a population of 35,000 people, half of whom are French and a quarter Monagasque.
• Monaco is divided into four districts: Monaco-Ville, Condamine, Monte Carlo, and Fontvieille.
• It has been ruled by the Grimaldi family since 1215. Prince Rainier III has been figurehead since 1949.

GETTING THERE

It will be no surprise to you that the Monaco Grand Prix is an exclusive event, and exclusive means expensive. Tickets are in great demand but available if you book early enough via www.acm.mc as well as the usual ticket hawkers and travel agents. Expect to pay upwards of $500 for a grandstand ticket and $60 for the cheap seats. (Or bring your own seats and picnic on the sloped banks of the Secteur Rocher above *Anthony Noghes* corner.)

Accommodations will be tough to find, unless you have a wealthy buddy who owns a yacht.

If you're making your own way there, fly to Nice Cote d'Azur, the nearest airport, roughly 23 miles from Monaco. Take a bus straight from the airport to Monaco and you can be drinking cocktails at the Café de Paris next to the Casino de Monte Carlo within 40 minutes.

RACE WEEKEND

If you want the whole experience, be sure to be there from the start, for the practice sessions and the fights for pole position in the crucial qualifying sessions on Saturday morning. Winning a good grid position is vital at Monaco, which makes the qualifying sessions a must-see.

THE DRIVERS

Winning the Monaco Grand Prix places you in the realm of true champions. Although not the most comfortable of races—conditions are cramped for pit crews as well as for drivers—the stars of the show dream of following in the steps of the greats. Monaco winners Ayrton Senna, Michael Schumacher, and "Mr. Monaco" himself, Graham Hill, are just three of the sport's heroes who have inspired and entertained in the race's great history. It's at Monaco that ambition burns red as the lights turn green.

All Formula One drivers are incredible athletes, their bodies honed to endure anything up to a sustained 3.5 G of cornering force. High-tech indoor gyms that simulate changes in temperature and altitude are used for training and building endurance. Cardiovascular training improves endurance, while the neck muscles are worked on to withstand the force and acceleration of the car in practice and race conditions. If you've been go-karting for even 30 minutes, you'll know the strain that steering puts on your forearms. Imagine what controlling a Formula One car around a 3.4-kilometer circuit for two hours at speeds in excess of 175 mph would be like without the required training.

THE HISTORY

The first Monaco Grand Prix was held on April 14, 1929, at 1:30 p.m. Since then, the fastest average race speed has risen from 50 mph to 96 mph. The race is organized every year by the Automobile Club de Monaco.

THE OUTFIT

A Grand Prix driver's clothing is state of the art and competes in the coolness stakes with a fighter pilot's uniform. Modern suits are fireproof, undergoing intense flame testing to ensure safety standards are met. Although fires in the modern sport are rare, suits are designed to withstand extreme temperatures and, if trapped in a burning car, a driver will remain protected until rescued. Overalls are extremely light and allow the skin to breathe while absorbing sweat induced by the heat, which during the summer months can be excessive and incapacitating even to those wearing shorts. Two fabric handles on the shoulders of each suit allow marshals or pit crews to pull the driver from his seat in case of emergency.

The Formula One helmet is designed much like any other protective headgear, to guard against major impact. But built into each helmet is also a car-to-pit communication device, and liquid intake tubes to ensure the drivers remain hydrated. Drinking before and during competition compensates for the seven pounds of sweat they can lose during the race.

Affixed to the helmet visor are thin, transparent sheets of plastic that the drivers can tear off during the race, so that their sight is not obscured by rain, dirt, or oil from other cars.

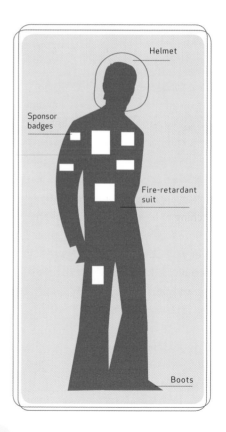

Helmet

Sponsor badges

Fire-retardant suit

Boots

NEGOTIATING THE ULTIMATE STREET COURSE

"It goes without saying that the track is made up entirely of ends, steep uphill climbs and fast downhill runs. Any respectable traffic system would have covered the track with 'Danger' sign posts left, right and center."

—La Vie Automobile, 1929

To say the Monaco Grand Prix is challenging is an understatement. The narrow, winding streets of Monte Carlo make overtaking another car nearly impossible. Those who try risk serious injury. But the allure of speed does strange things to the brain, and this adds to the thrill of watching at Monaco. Outmaneuvering opponents is of course what a Grand Prix driver gets paid for. It's also what spectators pay to watch, and the proximity of the fans to the cars gives extra bang for your buck.

On the grid, the drivers wait patiently for the warm-up lap. They are entirely focused on the 78 laps that will require their total concentration. The track, weather conditions, and competition have been assessed and, based on these, decisions have been made on the tire compound to be used and the fuel load at the start of the race. A strong race strategy is critical and will decide the race winner and losers.

As the engines start, the sound is immense. The screaming and whining of engines drown out the cheers of those standing behind the barricades, in the stands, or leaning from balconies above the track. The drivers begin the warm-up lap, showing off their machines like untamed beasts, heating up the brakes and tires. They then return to their grid positions to fix their eyes on the lights ahead.

Silence as the crowd, the pit crew, the world's media, and TV viewers hold their breath for the green lights. And it's GO!

HITCHING A RIDE WITH GIANCARLO FISICHELLA:

"The lap starts on the pit straight where I will reach over 270 kph (165 mph) in sixth gear, before braking to second gear and

around 86 kph (50 mph) for the Sainte Devote corner.

From here I accelerate up the long hill reaching about 260 kph (160 mph) before going into the long left-hand third gear corner Massenet, which leads to the famous Casino corner.

I remain in third gear for this and take it at around 120 kph (75 mph), and as I crest the hill the car becomes very light and slides toward the barrier. Then there's a very bumpy, highly cambered straight on which the car reaches around 210 kph (130 mph), and which leads down to the first of the first gear hairpins, the Mirabeau hairpin, which is taken at under 70 kph (45 mph).

There's a very short period of acceleration which leads down to the tightest of all the corners at Monaco, the Grand (formerly Loews) hairpin, which again is taken in first gear and the speed can be as low as 45 kph (30 mph).

The downhill stretch leads to Portier, which in turn leads in to the Tunnel, both of which are taken in second gear at under 80 kph (50 mph). As you enter the tunnel it's quite tricky because you not only have

to get used to a change in the ambient light, but there is also quite a difficult corner in the tunnel which is taken at over 250 kph (155 mph) in top gear.

On exiting the tunnel, braking is very difficult for the chicane—an artificial barrier or obstacle on the race course—as you are heading downhill and have to brake from the maximum speed on the circuit of 280 kph (170 mph) down to around 60 kph (45 mph) and first gear for the Harbour Chicane.

From here I will reach around 225 kph (140 mph) before going through the Tabac corner in fourth gear at around 160 kph (100 mph). I remain in fourth gear for the first, fast part of the Swimming Pool, before braking to second gear and 80 kph (50 mph) for the second part.

The approach to the final hairpin, Rascasse, is very difficult as you have to brake from around 185 kph (115 mph) while still on a curve, down to 50 kph (35 mph) for this first gear corner.

On exiting this corner it is very difficult to control the wheel spin as you accelerate up to the final corner, Anthony Noghes, which is taken at around 75 kph (45 mph) in second gear.

The lap then finishes on the pit straight."

—Giancarlo Fisichella, Sauber-Petronas,—an excerpt from an interview with www.planet-f1.com

So now Giancarlo has given you his view of the track. You can also experience it yourself by taking a law-abiding spin around the course after the race. Bear in mind that you're unlikely to do it as well as a Formula One driver. So if you throw your four-cylinder hatchback round *Rascasse* and approach *Tabac* in fourth gear, you're likely to crash or be thrown in to a jail.

LEARN MORE

Book your tickets early at www.acm. mc. For more of the best and latest Grand Prix results and background, go to www.planet-f1.com and www. formula1.com.

THE HORROR STORIES

One mistake at Monaco can end in tragedy, and almost has for some drivers. On May 12, 1994, Karl Wendlinger, the Austrian Sauber driver, braked too late exiting the *Tunnel* in a practice session. He smashed into the chicane barriers at 125 mph. The horrendous crash left Wendlinger in a deep coma, yet his incredible recovery meant he was racing again in 1995. He never regained the Formula One talent he had shown previously but he escaped with his life.

In 2003, 23-year-old British driver Jensen Button escaped injury after a practice lap crash at 180 mph. Button was knocked unconscious but was back to race in Canada two weeks later. Like a true racing hero, he put the crash behind him and a year later he was standing in second place on the Monaco 2004 Grand Prix podium.

FOR YOUR OWN SCRAPBOOK:

THE TOUR DE FRANCE

Thanks to the triumphs of Greg Le Mond and Lance Armstrong, Americans have become familiar with the Tour de France. If you vacation in France, you'll see groups of elderly men dressed in tight Lycra, rising at dawn and exercising their geriatric muscles until twilight. In the Alps you'll encounter mountain roads that are hard to drive up, let alone cycle up. Cycling is a physically demanding sport. It's a great advertisement for healthy living when 80-year-olds are still pounding the pedals well after they've received their state pension.

However, there's a lot more to the sport than just getting out on two wheels to admire the countryside. The Tour de France is testimony to that. This grueling competition has the best cyclists in the world battling to wear the famous yellow jersey. It has world-respected heroes, daunting distances, and, of course, very, very steep hills.

THE TOUR DE FRANCE—THE BASIC FACTS

WHAT: To win the Tour de France—the greatest bike race on earth—is every serious cyclist's dream. It's a true test of their technique as well as mental and physical strength.

WHERE: No surprises that this race is held predominantly in France. However, the competition has crossed the channel to England and started in the neighboring country, Belgium.

The race covers incredible distances and much of France, from Paris in the north to Bordeaux in the west. Up snow-capped mountains to sunflower-filled valleys, it seems there's nowhere these athletes don't go.

WHEN: Held over 21 days in July.

TOTAL DISTANCE: If you thought your Sunday bike ride was tiring, try cycling 2,100 miles over three weeks. There are 20 stages in total, with distances between 100 and 140 miles each.

WHO: 22 teams with nine riders per team, for a total of 198 riders. Many more people hold out water bottles, marshal, keep time, and tend to the exhausted.

HOW: Entry is by invitation only.

HOW MANY: Vast numbers of people turn out to cheer the riders. An estimated 15 million line the streets over the three weeks with an incredible two billion viewers tuning in to global TV coverage. Seventy-five TV networks broadcast the Tour de France in more than 170 countries to create 2,400 hours of TV programming.

To win a stage of the Tour de France can be the highlight of a cyclist's career. This notoriously competitive race requires each rider to be at the peak of physical fitness in order to cover the distance and make his mark.

THE COMPETITIONS

To add some diversity to this mammoth competition, a cyclist in the Tour de France will encounter different types of racing as he plows his way through the French towns, cities, and countryside.

MASS START: Typical of most of the 20 stages of the Tour. Riders all start together to cover a specific route taking them from one town to another. The largest group of riders, who remain together during the trial, is known as the *peloton*. The winner of the stage is the first rider to cross the finish line.

INDIVIDUAL TIME TRIAL (ITT):

Approximately three stages of the Tour de France are run as individual time trials. Riders start independently of each other to cover the specified route and are timed, making this is a good chance to either increase the lead or to *avoir des fourmis dans les jambes* (translated as *to have ants in your legs*). The fastest is the winner of this stage.

TEAM TIME TRIAL (TTT): Another component of the Tour de France is the Team Time Trial stage. Like the ITT, it's fastest to the line. However, all members of a team start together and aim to ride together over the whole course, as every member will be given the same time if they cross the line in a group. Straying team members who don't finish in their group will be timed independently.

THE STAKES

Winning the Yellow Jersey (the famous Maillot Jaune)

The General Classification assesses the cumulative total over all the stages of the Tour de France. The leader of the General Classification at the end of a stage (the rider with the lowest cumulative time) wears the yellow jersey the following day. It's the jersey every rider wants to be photographed wearing.

Winning the Green Jersey

The Points Competition awards points to those who finish the stages in the top 20. The winner of a mass start stage earns up to 35 points. The leader of the Points Competition gets to wear the coveted green jersey.

Winning the Red Polka Dot Jersey

King of the Mountains is not a bad name to have. Some stages finish at the summits of the Alps or Pyrenees, and after winning these stages you deserve this grand title. Each of these mountain climbs is graded from a Sunday cycle, Grade 4, to a day in hell, Grade 1. And if you thought nothing could be worse than hell, there's *hors categorie* (out of category), the name given to the nastiest climbs of them all, including the fearsome *Alpe d'Huez* (usually best ascended by chairlift). The tougher the climb, the more points you receive.

Winning the White Jersey

For the highest placed General Classification rider less than 25 years of age, there's a white jersey up for grabs.

THE RULES IN BRIEF

Although not an exhaustive list, these are some of the rules you'll need to adhere to in order to avoid getting thrown out of the competition:

Riders' Identification

Number plates must be attached to the front of the bicycle frames, and riders must wear two rider numbers on their right and left hips.

Technical Assistance

Riders may help one another in minor circumstances (exchanging food, drinks, or accessories). Exchanging tires, wheels, or bicycles is only permitted among riders from the same team.

Food

In general, food is permitted at any time starting from the 50-km (about 31-mile) distance marker of a stage up to the distance marker indicating "end of feeding" (20 km [about 12.5 miles] from the finish).

Infraction en Course

Drafting behind a car, pushing, pulling, and holding on are all strictly forbidden.

Timing

For the ITT, a rider must leave a gap of at

least 2 meters (about 6.5 feet) between himself and any rider he passes. A rider caught up by another rider will stay at least 25 meters (about 82 feet) behind the latter.

Team Vehicles

A rider may be accompanied by a vehicle carrying spares and offering emergency aid. The vehicle must remain 10 meters (about 33 feet) behind its rider; it may never draw level with him and all information must be communicated from its position behind the rider. Most cyclists now wear two-way communicators that make screaming from speeding cars obsolete.

THE HISTORY

The idea of a major cycling race covering the perimeter of France was conceived by a publication called *L'Auto* in 1903. Originally a marketing ploy to boost

circulation, as the prize money increased and daily expenses were offered to cyclists, the appeal grew. After aborted attempts to get the race organized, 60 riders finally took to the roads on July 19, 1903. As a result, *L'Auto* sold more than 130,000 copies of their publication, more than 100,000 more than they had sold six months earlier.

The race was a success and in 1919 the yellow jersey made its first appearance. Over its history the prize purse has increased from approximately $1,700 to $2.1 million.

THE ROUTE

The stages in the first 5 to 10 days of the Tour de France are relatively flat. However, later in the Tour, stages quickly become more demanding and involve the grueling mountain climbs.

GET ON YOUR BIKE

For those who take their cycling seriously but haven't quite made the big time, why not do the Tour de France yourself? Completing the stages before the big names roll into town, you'll not only have the personal satisfaction of having been

there but your blisters, saddle sores, and photo album will also prove that you've done it.

LEARN MORE

To find out more, visit www.letour.fr. Plunk down some cash and ride the race route yourself; try www.eurocycler.com.

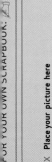

X **Place your picture here**

THE HAHNENKAMM—A DOWNHILL LEGEND

The Hahnenkamm holds a special place in skiing history. It's the most notorious downhill race on the skiing calendar and makes even the hardiest and most determined of professional skiers quake in their ski boots.

The course is perilous to the novice skier, and without technique, skill, and luck, you might well get to the bottom of the run via stretcher.

Afraid? Of course not.

HAHNENKAMM—THE BASIC FACTS

WHAT: The Hahnenkamm is a combined race involving a downhill run, *the Streif*, and a slalom course, *Ganslern*.

WHERE: Kitzbühel, a world-renowned resort situated in the Austrian Tyrolean mountains.

WHEN: Three days in late January.

WHY: The race is a true test of steel and skill for any of the world's best skiers. Past winners have shown dexterity and nerve, and those with faith thank their holy maker that they made it to the bottom in one piece.

WHO: The Hahnenkamm, a key race, is skied every year (with a few exceptions due to poor snow conditions) by the sport's greatest.

They compete in the downhill, Super-G, and slalom to win the ultimate accolade as winner of the Hahnenkamm. It's the skier with the fastest combined total time who becomes the traditional Hahnenkamm champion.

More than 1,000 people are involved in the organizing of Hahnenkamm race days, which are directed by the Kitzbüheler Ski Club.

HOW: To be a participant in the main race of the season, you'll have to ski like a god, be a member of a national ski team, and possess an incredible amount of confidence. Add to that the prayers of a whole nation and you're nearly qualified. You can race it yourself the day after the competition. But you'll need permission and race skis to grip the icy surface.

HOW MUCH: To watch the Hahnenkamm, get there early and be prepared to pay about $18 to $73, depending on the view. You'll be joined by nearly 100,000 screaming fans, from the jetsetters to ski bums.

HOW TO GET THERE: Fly to either Innsbruck, Austria, or to Munich, Germany, where you can get direct trains into Kitzbühel station.

THE HAHNENKAMM—IN MORE DETAIL

Positioned at the top of the *Streif*, your brain and legs conspire against you. Your brain is yelling, "Don't do it!" Your legs are screaming, "We like the way we look; please keep us in one piece!" It's not even as if you can slide down this mighty hill on your backside, unless you want to be plagued by hemorrhoids for the rest of your life. Suddenly the restaurant at the top of the course looks extremely appealing.

So what is the attraction? Flying through the air on skis at nearly 90 mph.

THE HISTORY

The first international Hahnenkamm race was in 1931. Its champion, Austrian Ferdl Friedensbacher, skied the course in 4 minutes, 34 seconds. The 2004 winner, fellow countryman Stephan Eberharter, skied the course in 1 minute, 55 seconds.

In 1967 the first Alpine World Cup took place with the Hahnenkamm runs as its main focus. In its 73-year history, the races have only been cancelled three times (1964, 1988, and 1993) because of poor snow conditions. Now, snow machines ensure that the race continues to challenge the best, year after year.

THE STREIF

Racing the *Streif* takes no more than two minutes for today's world-class professional. The 2-mile descent is treacherously icy and incredibly difficult to get an edge on. Racers reach speeds of 87 mph as they negotiate drops of 85 degrees and jumps of 262 feet. From the start of the race, the course plummets downhill and the racer with it. If you lose control, there's no place to slow down. Once you've started, you have no choice but to keep going, unless flying into the safety nets is your preferred emergency route. But then, at *Streif* speeds, safety nets definitely don't guarantee safety.

The winner in 2003 and the runner-up in 2004, Daron Rahlves of California talks through the course sections and sheds some light on how to hang in there:

THE START

"I just try to collect myself in that little moment I have before I head on course. You can feel some excitement, some tension, a lot of energy. I'll be breathing hard, trying to get as much wind in my lungs as I can. That fires me up a little more. Let's see what we've got for the race."

MAUSEFALLE

"Out of the start you kick out hard, skating to get some speed in the first turn. This is where you see where the guys really want to win, what they're doing up there, if they're looking for it, and you throw yourself into the next turn before Mausefalle."

KARUSELLKURVE

"The Karusellkurve is a pretty tricky turn. You have to figure out whether to slide the top of it and get the skis directed in the way you want to go or to try to arc the whole thing, which is a little tougher to do."

STEILHANG

"Coming into the Steilhang it takes a switch from your left ski in the air to your right ski—it's like a 90-degree turn down the really steep pitch. This is the most important section for me coming onto the flats."

STEILHANG TO BRÜECKENSCHUSS

"Once you drop off the Steilhang you have what you've got, and you just have to hold a good tuck. Aerodynamics is important. It goes straight ahead and banks left pretty quickly onto a really flat road."

ALTESCHNEISSE TO SEIDELALM

"The Alteschneisse is the end of the flats. You drop off by the gate and point it straight and hang on to the right ski a little bit trying to make as much speed as you can going into the next section by the Seidelalm."

LEARN MORE
Visit www.kitzbuehel.com.

SEIDELALMSPRUNG

"Coming into the Seidelalmsprung you land straight down this hill, switch to the left ski, and come over a little roller, which is a pretty good feeling, you just get light, you switch to your right ski in the air and try to put it down as clean as you can."

LÄERCHENSCHUSS

"The Läerchenschuss is a long turn on your left ski so you really try to squeak out as much speed as you can—so you try to drag it out just the last couple inches before the next gate. You take a lot of speed into the Oberhausberg."

OBERHAUSBERG

"This section is just trying to maintain your speed. It has a little quick chicane in it from the right, left-to-right-foot turn. Then you come into this sidehill right-footer, setting yourself up for the Hausbergkante."

HAUSBERGKANTE

"It's really tough here, gnarly—this is what traditional downhill is all about and why Kitzbühel is so feared. To me, this is where it separates the men from the boys, the good from the best, and this is where you get that ultimate feeling of flying down a course on skis."

ZEILSCHUSS

"You basically just fight for speed down there. There's a compression at the bottom of that and definitely try to stay up on your feet on that one. And then straight off the jump and into the finish ... phew."

—Excerpt from an interview with Daron Rahlves, www.usskiteam.com

THE KITZBÜHEL GREATS

It can only be fair to say that anyone who skis the entire length of the Hahnenkamm is a "great." Before the race, a number of skiers prepare the line of the course for the competitors to follow on race day. They get little credit but have the satisfaction of knowing they've carved their mark on the mountain that hosts the most awesome runs in the sport of skiing.

Those who win the race itself become legends, with their name and the flag of their nation painted on the gondolas that glide you up the mountain. The king of the Hahnenkamm is undoubtedly race legend Franz Klammer, the Austrian who has won four times.

THE APRÈS SKI

For some, the après ski is what skiing is all about: after a few hours hacking through ice and snow, spend an afternoon, evening, and early morning downing schnapps, mulled wine, or beer.

Race days in Kitzbühel are certainly no exception. Every night is party night. The heroes of Hahnenkamm enter the heaving bars in their gladiatorial splendor and are greeted by a beer drenching. The relief of having made it down the hill leads to

an alcohol-fueled night. Dancing, singing, drinking, and falling over ensue as night turns to morning—time for the lift-pass paying public to try out the king of the pistes for themselves.

BUNGEE JUMPING

James Bond's dive from the dizzying heights of a Russian dam has been voted the best movie stunt of all time. Undoubtedly an amazing act of courage, this scene, in the opening minutes of the film *Goldeneye*, continues to stun audiences worldwide.

Bungee jumping is a slightly kamikaze pastime, but for those seeking one of the biggest natural highs (and lows), this is a sport that can provide it all—within seconds.

BUNGEE JUMPING—THE BASIC FACTS

WHAT: The physics of bungee jumping primarily involves the conversion of gravitational potential energy into the elastic energy of a stretched bungee cord. In other words, your lifeline is a big elastic band, the only thing stopping you from prematurely meeting your maker.

WHERE: The *Goldeneye* dive was actually filmed at the Verzasca Dam in the Swiss Italian region of Ticino. The dam is located in the wilds of the Verzasca Valley, not far from Locarno. And for those with a strong stomach, it's the ideal place to find the adventure of a lifetime.

WHEN: The best time to jump is in late spring or early summer, when you can experience the breathtaking local beauty without having to wear seven layers of warm clothing. You'll need to book well in advance, as this is now a location on many people's radar.

HOW HIGH: A highly terrifying 722 feet.

HOW TO GET THERE: You can reach Locarno by train from Bellinzona, the capital of the Ticino region, in 30 minutes. A local bus will take you into the Valle Verzasca.

BUNGEE JUMPING—IN MORE DETAIL

Bungee jumping is an incredible feat, if you have the nerve to carry it off. There are stunning locations around the world where you can leap from bridges, buildings, or cranes, while experiencing incredible views both in front of and below you. Ensuring that the organizers are experienced and using the right equipment is essential. After all, you're putting your life in their hands.

As you make it to the top of the dam, your heart is pounding, your stomach already doing somersaults, and blood is pumping around your body like a rabbit around a greyhound track. Already attached to the bungee cord, you prepare yourself for the exuberant swan dive that will impress your friends. The dam is an incredible feat of engineering, with banked walls and a verdant forest backdrop.

With an intake of breath, you launch from the platform over a drop of seemingly incomparable height. You hurtle toward the ground for a full 7-second free fall, experiencing an almighty rush of adrenaline. The cord dutifully prevents an untimely death and, surprisingly, doesn't snap you back aggressively, instead pulling you smoothly into its floating, slackened coils. The rebound subsides; you close your eyes, grinning from ear to ear. Thank God, you're still alive.

THE HISTORY

Bungee was first practiced centuries ago in Vanuatu in the South Pacific, where today the tradition is still a rite of passage from youth to manhood. As each young man ascends into the treetops and walks onto the jumping platform 50 feet above the ground, the crowd below dances and chants in encouragement. He quiets them and speaks a few, poignant last words before the jump. Vines are wrapped around his ankles, and the crowd begins to chant, encouraging him to jump. He steps forward onto the platform above and

leans forward, the action smooth
and graceful until the vines snap taut,
rescuing him from the earth's jaws just
5 feet from impact.

Since being discovered by the Western
world, bungee jumping has taken off.
There are now clubs in thousands of
locations, some natural, others man-
made—both types providing a pure and
natural rush of energy and excitement.

LEARN MORE

To find out more about safety codes and
equipment, contact the NABA (North
American Bungee Association) at
www.bungee.com. Like us, they'll advise
you to ensure that you jump safely with
the assistance of qualified instructors.

JUMPING METHODS

Some people just can't commit.

Standing in the middle of a bridge with a
canyon of white, foaming rapids below is
a scary place to be. It can be difficult to
find the motivation to throw yourself off,
which is why some people volunteer to
place their trust in an instructor's hands
and be pushed.

However, for a more impressive once-in-
a-lifetime stunt, you can use the following
techniques.

Swan Dive

This is the jump to satisfy the James Bond
in you. You take one look down, admire the
view, and leap from the platform, arms
stretched wide and to your sides. You dive
through the air like a bird locked onto its
earthbound target.

Back Dive

Positioned with your back turned on the
edge of the platform, you throw yourself
into a backwards dive. You make a full arc

with your body so that from your initial leap you are now pointing straight down toward the ground.

Bat Drop

Perhaps for your first jump you're not ready to throw yourself off the platform like a gung ho marine. Instead you require qualified assistance, someone to lower you head-first from the platform so you're hanging just below it looking at the ground below. The count begins. Three, two, one . . . Hello Earth.

Water Touchdown

You might feel like asking to see the calculations on this one. The organizers are confident that your jump will be so accurate that you'll dunk your head in the water below before being pulled back by the bungee cord. If you try this, make sure the water's deep.

NEW YORK MARATHON

You've been training for this race for six months. You've abstained from alcohol while watching your friends chug beers and shots in the bar after work. You've (semi) resisted the full-fat versions of your favorite foods while everyone else around you has been eating like pigs at a trough.

In addition you've spent your hard-earned cash on state-of-the-art running shoes, clothes, and enough electronic gadgetry to monitor your heartbeat, your average speed, and your location via GPS technology.

Now it's your time. The day of the New York Marathon has arrived.

NEW YORK MARATHON—THE BASIC FACTS

WHERE: NYC, the Big Apple. The marathon will take its participants through the city's five boroughs and over five bridges.

WHEN: First Sunday in November.

WHAT: 26.2 miles of hard slog through the streets of New York.

HOW: To get a guaranteed place, you have to get your entry form in by the published deadline. If you're not in time, your place can be obtained through the club's lottery system.

WHO: The local mailman, a guy wearing a wet suit complete with aqualung, a girl with a mountain bike hung over her shoulder, a retired librarian from Milwaukee, a Brooklyn padre. This is a race run by the broadest cross-section of human life. And with 35,000 people running in the 2004 marathon, you can bet there'll be at least one fella running as Big Bird from *Sesame Street*.

HOW MUCH: For U.S. residents, the entry fee will set you back about $80.

This is the premier event of New York Road Runners, and on marathon day New York is a party city. Central Park and Fifth Avenue are buzzing with bands playing for runners, their friends and families, and spectators—all adding to the carnival atmosphere. The week before the race is the time for New Yorkers to shape up as half marathons and organized runs fill up the diary as the big 26-miler approaches.

THE HISTORY

With only $1,000 available for organizers to play with, the first marathon in 1970 was a far lower-key affair than today's equivalent. Just 55 people finished the race. However, the popularity of the marathon has grown impressively ever since. In 1976, about 2,000 people ran a new course through Central Park, and by 1995, 27,000 runners crossed the finish line.

The year 2001 was a particularly poignant landmark in the marathon's history. Following the terrorist attack on the World Trade Center, a record number of New Yorkers took to the streets to demonstrate their pride in their city and show solidarity in the wake of the disaster.

The next year, nearly 32,000 finished the marathon. Within just over two decades, it has become the most famous marathon in the world.

LEARN MORE
To get your entry in, head to www.ingnycmarathon.org.

THE ROUTE

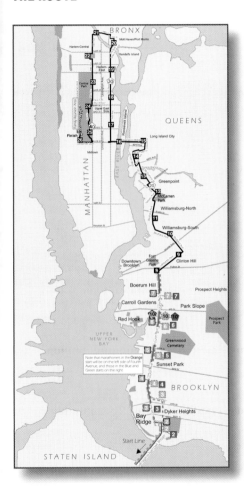

(c) New York Road Runners Club Inc.

The marathon is a sightseeing tour you'll have to work very hard for.

The race carries its runners through all five boroughs: Staten Island, Brooklyn, Queens, the Bronx, and Manhattan. They'll also cross five bridges on an incredible journey through the cosmopolitan inner city and, for some, though the pain barrier.

At the starting line on Staten Island, 35,000 runners lurch across, heading straight over the expansive Verrazano Bridge into Brooklyn. A change of direction takes the runners into Queens, over the bridge, and into Manhattan. If you're among them, you're in pain; your legs are burning and screaming at you to stop. But the cheers of the Fifth Avenue crowds carry you, spurring you on, and you feel fresh exhilaration that, although ephemeral, may just get you through the last 4 miles through Central Park and over the finish line.

Remember, there's an eight-and-a-half-hour time limit to run the course, so it's not the time to stop off at Bloomingdale's to do some shopping.

INDIANAPOLIS 500
—"GENTLEMEN, START YOUR ENGINES"

Auto racing has always been a dangerous occupation, but the sophistication of modern technology and engineering has saved the lives of many participants over the last decade. The Indy 500 is a competition that has had more than its fair share of fatalities, but the danger and uncertainty of the sport are what attracts so many to it. This is an event any adrenaline-junkie won't want to miss. Every year, the Indy 500 holds spectators captive as their racing heroes climb into their cars to outclass each other and the legends who raced before them.

INDY 500—THE BASIC FACTS

WHERE: The race is held at the Indianapolis Motor Speedway, popularly known as The Brickyard. It's also host to the Brickyard 400 NASCAR race and the U.S. Formula One Grand Prix.

WHAT: This is the most anticipated annual U.S. auto race. It's the fourth race in the season's 16-race series.

WHEN: The Indy 500 is milked for all its worth and takes up a good chunk of the month of May. You've got to truly love the Indy 500 (and have a lot of vacation to take) to want to attend every day of this festival, which starts around May 9 and continues to the end of the month. From fashion shows to a half marathon to parades, this is an event for all the family. For the true racing enthusiast, the key days to note are:

- Pole qualifying—some two weeks before the race
- Bump Day qualifying—one week before the race
- Carb Day—three days before the race
- Race Day—the big one, noon (EDT) Sunday of Memorial Day Weekend

WHO: There are traditionally 33 drivers and their cars permitted to compete on race day for the Borg-Warner Trophy. And it's not just men who take part. Three women have raced in the Indianapolis 500 to date: Janet Guthrie (1977–79), Lyn St. James (1992–97, 2000), and Sarah Fisher, who continues to attempt to beat the boys to the checkered flag. And, no, you won't find them applying lipstick in the rearview mirror.

HOW MANY PEOPLE: The Speedway has a vast capacity and on a crowded race day your grinning face will be just one of as many as 300,000.

NUMBER OF LAPS: 200 laps of a 2.5-mile circuit (hence the Indy 500).

FASTEST TIME: 237.498 mph was recorded by Arie Luyendyk during qualifying on May 12, 1996.

HOW MUCH: Nonrace days won't set you back a fortune. However, to watch the Indy 500 itself, you'll need to cough up $70. If you truly want to splurge, you could punk down $800 for the hottest seats.

Want to buy into the thrill of it all? You'll need wealth, luck, and an open wallet. Taking part in the Indy 500 alone will cost you approximately $10,000 for each driver entry. Budget another $1 million per car while you're there. Of course, you'll already have spent millions on a car, a driver, and the team of

mechanics and engineers that keep you and your drivers mobile throughout the season. And you won't need to worry about sponsorship as you'll have already struck up lucrative deals with major U.S. corporations.

HOW TO GET THERE: You'll find the Indianapolis Motor Speedway to the west of the city and a very short distance from Indianapolis International Airport. It's easily accessible by car.

Somehow it's not surprising that even a century ago, young men were tinkering in their garages, tuning their motors for the big race, a soft porn calendar of the era hung on the wall. Fulfilling the urge to throw a car around a track is just part of the male make-up. And, some women's too. Since the 1970s, women have been competing, proving you don't just need balls of steel to get in an Indy car cockpit and overcome memories of those who have sadly never made it out of theirs.

THE HISTORY

The Indianapolis Motor Speedway was

founded by Carl Fisher in 1906. The track was built in 1909 and the first attempt at a race here resulted in tragedy with the deaths of two drivers, two mechanics, and two spectators. Thus it wasn't until 1911 that the first Indy 500 was actually raced.

Since 1946, there has been an Indy 500 race every year, despite the political wrangling between rival racing teams, deaths, and inclement weather conditions.

Long-standing feuds between proponents of different race formats caused tension in the 1990s, but the sport's strong following ensured its success.

In 1957, the 500 Festival was organized to celebrate The Greatest Spectacle in Racing. Parades and pageants continue to sweep through the city during the Indy 500 month of May.

THE COURSE

The Indy 500 track is 2.5 miles around, and drivers can turn a lap in about 40 seconds.

This circuit is oval and made from asphalt.

The track is also accustomed to enduring some serious damage: burning rubber and burning cars.

The layout of the course has remained unchanged since 1909, with four turns. The front and back straightaways are five-eighths of a mile, with the shorts at one-eighth of a mile each. Each of the four turns is a quarter mile long. Compared to the average Formula One track, it doesn't look particularly challenging. However, combine positional warfare on the banked shorter straightaways and the fight for speed on the long straightaways and you have one very exciting race on your hands.

In 1911, the average speed around the course was 75 mph. Today, drivers risk their lives (and sometimes those of the spectators) driving at average speeds of 180 mph and top speeds of 230 mph. The

LEARN MORE
You'll find all the very latest Indy 500 stats and figures at www.indy500.com.

Indy 500 is arguably the best example of the gut-wrenching brutality of high-speed auto racing. (Just don't tell that to the Formula One devotee.)

BIG NAMES IN THE INDY 500

The first driver to win the Indy 500 was Ray Harroun, who in 1911 completed the race in six hours and 42 minutes, driving at an average speed of 75 mph. In the 1940s, Wilbur Shaw, three-time race winner and

A.J. Foyt, Rick Mears, and Al Unser each won the race four times, followed by such modern-day champions as Emerson Fittipaldi and Helio Castroneves. Fittipaldi was the first driver to win more than $1 million for a single race. In 2002 the prize purse reached $10 million for the first time in the race's history, proving that those who defy death should be rewarded handsomely for it (and would be wise to spend it before their next Indy 500).

INDY TRAGEDY

With speed, metal, and untethered human ambition at the very heart of Indy car racing, it's no wonder that in its lifetime, the Indy 500 has sadly ended many lives. Drivers, team members, and spectators who have been killed at the event are remembered by all who hold the Indy 500 close to their hearts. This is a sport that has its heroes, both past and present, and never forgets those who died on its hallowed ground. But despite these memories and the dangers faced by those involved, once hooked, the passion for the Indy 500 is hard to shake.

president and general manager of the Indianapolis Motor Speedway, coined the phrase "Gentlemen, start your engines" to get everyone's hearts pounding in time to the revving of engines.

"Triathlon is no longer a hobby, it's become, well... it's become a lifestyle."
—John Collins, the Ironman inventor, 1998

Sitting comfortably, Doritos and dip perched conveniently on the sofa arm, a cold beer in one hand and a remote in the other, a triathlon seems less of a hobby than a suicidal bid to invoke cardiac arrest. Never mind the two packets of chips and six-pack you've already consumed.

Contests certainly don't come much tougher than the Ironman. If you're inspired enough, put down the beer, pick up a Gatorade and offer your poorly toned body and soul to a personal trainer. You'll need to put in serious hours to be fit enough to run, cycle, and swim a combined 140 miles. Make it through the initial qualifying sessions, and you'll join a bunch of supremely fit individuals, all pushing their bodies to the limits to attain the coveted title of men's and women's World Champion Ironman.

HAWAIIAN IRONMAN WORLD CHAMPIONSHIP — THE BASIC FACTS

WHERE: Although the first Ironman event was on Oahu, in 1981 its new home became Kailua-Kona, on Hawaii's big island. The island boasts great weather all year-round—great if you're vacationing, but a bit steamy if you're running in temperatures of up to 95°F.

WHAT: The Ironman triathlon event is a grueling 140-mile challenge: a 26-mile marathon, a 112-mile cycle and a 2.4-mile swim. The cut-off time is 17 hours.

WHEN: Held in mid-October.

WHO: Some 1,600 athletes from more than 50 countries participated in what was the triathlon's 25th year (2003). In addition, 50 million viewers worldwide watched the feats from the comfort of their armchairs.

HOW OLD: The beauty of Ironman is in the makeup of its competitors, men and women of all ages. In 1994, at the age of 77, Jim Ward became the oldest athlete to complete the course within the cut-off time. Age-group champions automatically qualify for the following year's event.

HOW: To take part on the big day, you'll need to have succeeded in one of the 25 qualifying events worldwide. Either that or you can enter a lottery. But even if you snag one of the 150 places available through the U.S. lottery system, you still need to prove that you've run, cycled, or swum at least half the distances demanded of you on the big day.

HOW MUCH: The entry fee for the Ironman World Championship is a little over $450. Not a bad value considering you'll have the kudos of telling your buddies (and more importantly, the opposite sex) that you've competed in one of the world's toughest sporting events.

TIMES TO BEAT: If you think you've got what it takes to win, carefully consider the distances, your own personal bests, and your particular strengths and weaknesses. Add a possible 60 mph cross wind into the equation and the small issue of the world record, set by Luc Van Lierde in 1996 at 8 hours, 4 minutes, and 8 seconds, and by Paula Newby-Fraser in 1992 at 8 hours, 55 minutes, and 28 seconds. Still feeling confident, or have you given in to the temptation of the beer and chips?

THE PRIZE MONEY: $100,000 for first place and $30,000 for second. The overall prize purse is $430,000.

HOW TO GET THERE: Kailua-Kona is located in Hawaii County on Hawaii (known as the Big Island). It's between Kealakekua and Honokohau along Highway 11, near Holualoa, Keauhou, and the Kaloko-Honokohau National Historic Park.

HAWAIIAN IRONMAN WORLD CHAMPIONSHIP
—IN MORE DETAIL

The Ironman contest has deservedly caught the attention of the public and the media. We admire the stamina and resilience of the athletes and wish our own bodies could endure the same pounding.

THE HISTORY

In 1978, John Collins, a Navy commander, challenged a group of swimmers, runners, and cyclists to prove which discipline's athletes were the fittest. After much chest beating, a competition combining all three sports was organized, with the winner to be declared the Ironman. Fifteen men

entered the race and 12 completed it. Gordon Haller became the first Ironman after completing the course in 11 hours and 46 minutes. The race was perfect for him as he had no one specialty—he had all three.

By 1980, the Ironman competition had seemingly awakened triathlon events from their slumber, and competitions began worldwide. ABC was invited to televise the annual Ironman contest. That year 106 men and two women participated.

In 1981 the event moved from Oahu to the Big Island, and 326 athletes competed, with many more cheering them on. John Howard, formerly an Olympic cyclist, became Ironman with a winning time of 9 hours and 38 minutes. Linda Sweeney won the women's event in 12 hours.

In only its first four years, Ironman became a sponsored event through a deal with Bud Light.

In 1983, the introduction of the 17-hour cut-off time and qualifications events for the main Kona competition made attending the event tougher, but invited a consistently higher caliber of athlete.

With competitor figures growing each year, the number of spectators also started to grow, thanks to U.S. television network support from ABC and, in 1991, NBC Sports.

Qualifying rounds are now held all over the world and the Ironman title has become one of the most coveted around the globe.

TRAINING

These guys have to work at being good. And so do you, if you want to even pretend you got off your couch and took part.

Consider the following before entering the qualification stages: Over a period of seven months prior to the events, you will need to consistently cover approximately 300 miles per week through a combination of cycling, running, and swimming. Specialists recommend an average of 18 to 22 hours of training per week to prepare for Ironman. Time to tell your boss you'll be taking seven months off work to fit it all in.

THE COURSE

The swim course is first up, with the participants running into the water at Kailua Pier. They will need to swim for 2.4

miles in crowded, 79°F, clear blue waters within a cut-off time of 2 hours and 20 minutes—so this is no time to bask in the beauty of the sea life clearly visible below. They pull their bodies from the Pacific waters at the same point they started. Although standing proves difficult for some, it's okay because the next part of the race is the cycling. The athletes quickly change from wet gear to dry cycling clothes and mount their bikes. They follow the Kona coast and onto the Kohala coast toward Hawi. This part of the triathlon has a cut-off time of 10 hours 30 minutes. It's not easy, especially as they cross "the wind-line" where gusts of up to 60 mph can blow them off their bikes.

Once the competitors have completed the grueling 112-mile cycle, it's onto their feet for the marathon, which they'll need to do in four and a half hours if they're to make the 17-hour cut-off.

They'll run through Kailua-Kona to Pahoehoe Park and on to Nelha, grabbing plenty of water along the way. Willing their bodies to break through the pain barrier, they complete the 26-mile race in Kailua-Kona running down Alii Drive to the finish line. The atmosphere at the finish line can be electric (unless you finish at 3:00 the next morning).

The professionals know they're doing badly if the glow sticks are handed out. As it gets dark, you'll know the winners and high rankers have long crossed the finish line. But anyone who completes this physically demanding race, inside or outside the cut-off time, will be rewarded abundantly by what is an incredible achievement.

X **Place your picture here**

LEARN MORE

Go to www.ironmanlive.com to find out how to take part.

FREE SOLOING—LEAVE THE ROPES AT HOME

"To those that have struggled with them, the mountains reveal beauties that they will not disclose to those who make no effort. That is the reward the mountains give to effort. And it is because they have so much to give and give it so lavishly to those who will wrestle with them that men love the mountains and go back to them again and again. The mountains reserve their choice gifts for those who stand upon their summits."

**—Sir Francis Younghusband
(British explorer, 1863—1942)**

Human endeavors to conquer the world's natural challenges are no more prolific than in the field of rock climbing. Climbing the world's biggest mountains has always been a source of great fascination and personal ambition. Free soloing presents a new challenge to climbers who have had traditional instruction but feel that their lives would not be complete without scaling the world's steepest rock faces devoid of the psychological comfort of being attached to ropes.

FREE SOLOING—THE BASIC FACTS

WHAT: Free soloing means climbing alone and without the security of ropes or climbing equipment. It's outdoor adventure at its most extreme: if you fall, you'll be lucky to escape with your life.

WHERE: Climbing in the United States is among the best in the world, with Yosemite National Park in California posing some of the biggest challenges to free soloing climbers. One of the most legendary sites is the sheer 3,000-foot granite face of Yosemite's El Capitan (known to its friends as El Cap).

WHEN: Anytime, but don't add the extra challenge of trying a free climb in the rain. Make sure the weather conditions are dry, warm, and bright just to give yourself a chance.

WHY: With risks this great, doing a climb of this nature can only be explained as personal choice. Free climbers talk about being at one with the rock and their body, having prepared mentally and physically for the challenge. This is a sport you cannot afford to take lightly, and only the most experienced climbers will be ready to embrace the challenge and fulfill it.

HOW: In your early climbing days, head to the gym or to a local indoor climbing wall where your every move is critiqued by a qualified instructor.

Once you've started a climb, pure concentration, determination, strength, and balance are all needed in equal amounts to ensure you make it to the top.

WHO: There's one name synonymous with free soloing and that's Lynn Hill. This 5-foot, 2-inch superwoman is the only person to have free climbed El Capitan's infamous Nose route. And she's done it twice.

EL CAP NOSE ROUTE RECORD: Lynn Hill holds the record for free climbing the El Cap Nose in 23 hours.

HOW MUCH: You'll need to fork out for a pair of climbing shoes. In some cases, for safety, you might want a harness and a belay device with locking carabiner. When your local climbing store identifies the equipment you need, the initial outlay will be a maximum of $400 (depending on how much of a designer snob you are).

FREE SOLOING—IN MORE DETAIL

A free climber depends entirely on footwork, agility, and physical and mental strength in order to succeed. Any use of equipment while ascending the rock face is called "aid" and, without this, the climber is purely at the mercy of the terrain and the elements.

The free climbing community is continually seeking new national and global challenges, making them a nomadic group of adventurers. Competition is usually friendly and, due to the sport's perilous nature, filled with mutual respect.

THE HISTORY

Over the last few decades, climbing technology and design have become more sophisticated, more effective, and therefore more widely used. As climbers became more aware of the negative effect they were having on the environment—rock faces scarred through use of pitons and other climbing aids, for example—a more natural form of climbing was needed to ensure ecological protection for the world's most frequented mountains. This drive for cleaner climbing saw the invention of less damaging equipment but also heralded an awakening of the desire to climb *au naturel*.

GRADING

If you're going to make any kind of claim to climbing a rock, you'll need to know what climbing grade you've achieved. The ratings system is a means of specifying the severity of a climb. Simply put:

1.0 = a flat and even surface
2.0 = a fairly flat surface with a slight gradient
3.0 = more of a scramble than a climb. Over rough terrain, you're not yet using your hands
4.0 = a rougher terrain needing a use of hands to maintain upward progression and stability
5.0 = rock climbing, using hands to climb a nearly vertical inclination

A rating of 5 is further broken down using the decimal system, getting more complex and difficult as the ratings increase. These can be further categorized by using a "+" or "−" and an A, B, C, or D grading with an additional rating number (for example 5.9 C1 is more complex along the scale). However, grading differs from country to country so it is always important to recheck before you climb in different regions around the world.

CLIMBING THE NOSE

The Nose is a completely direct route up El Cap. It is a difficult climb with aid, let alone without. At more than 2,850 feet in height, it demands superlative strength, stamina, and patience in order to master it successfully.

With a climbing grade of 5.13C or a 5.9A2 and more than 31 pitches of steep rock face, this is no climb for a novice.

Like early explorers charting unexplored oceans and lands, climbers map their routes, devising names for pitches, crevices, cracks, and maneuvers. They pass on their intelligence to fellow adventurers and climbing authorities to help others negotiate the ascent.

The Nose offers a great example of this as you climb from the *Stovelegs* (pitch 9) to the *Jardine Traverse* and on to the *Pancake Flake* and the notorious *Death block*. It's important to do your homework and know how to approach and overcome each of these obstacles. *The Great Roof* (pitch 22) is one of the Nose's key sections and demands such particular courage and balance that Hill coined the requisite move here—the *Houdini*.

It's important to look up and not just ahead. El Cap for most is a big climb and requires an overnight and overhead stay. There's always a chance you'll find climbers nesting like birds in their Portaledges, canopies that support and hang ominously from the rock face. With a four-day climb ahead of you, it's crucial to have somewhere to get your head down for the night and to be sheltered should the weather get a bit hairy.

CLIMBING—THE MOST BASIC ADVICE

These really are the basics so don't be crazy enough to rely on this information alone to get you mobile. Footwork is all important. You'll use your strong legs to push yourself up the route—pulling yourself up will just get you very tired very quickly.

You've bought the proper equipment, so use it. Your climbing shoes are designed to grip, so let them take the weight. Like any good climber you've tested your tools, tested them again, and then trust them like you trust your best friend.

LEARN MORE

For details on Yosemite activities and how to
get there, go to: www.nps.gov/yose

INDEX

PHOTO CREDITS